The Kindness of Strangers

THE KINDNESS OF STRANGERS

Oxfam is a registered charity in England and Wales (no 202918) and Scotland (SC039042).

An Hachette UK Company
www.hachette.co.uk

Summersdale Publishers Ltd
Part of Octopus Publishing Group Limited
Carmelite House
50 Victoria Embankment
LONDON
EC4Y 0DZ
UK

www.summersdale.com

Printed and bound by CPI Group (UK) Ltd, Croydon, CR0 4YY

ISBN: 978-1-78685-531-2

FSC
www.fsc.org
MIX
Paper from
responsible sources
FSC® C020471

Substantial discounts on bulk quantities of Summersdale books are available to corporations, professional associations and other organisations. For details contact general enquiries: telephone: +44 (0) 1243 771107 or email: enquiries@summersdale.com.

The views and opinions expressed in the stories contained herein belong solely to the editor and contributors and do not necessarily reflect the official policy or opinion of Oxfam GB nor have they been written on behalf of Oxfam GB.

Edited by
FEARGHAL O'NUALLAIN
Foreword by
LEVISON WOOD

The Kindness of Strangers

TRAVEL STORIES THAT MAKE YOUR HEART GROW

CONTENTS

STORIES THAT MAKE OUR HEARTS GROW

Foreword by Levison Wood

Over almost 20 years of travelling I've been lucky. I've been lucky to survive near misses; I've been lucky to escape danger; I've been lucky to come back in one piece. But I've also been lucky to make a great number of lifelong friends in the process from all around the world. Many of these friendships came about as a result of serendipity; chance encounters in random places. Conversations struck up on buses and in airports, over a drink in a bar or simply bumping into someone in the street. Even more, however, were formed when I was at my most vulnerable; when I was hitch-hiking, or sick, or in need of a bed for the night or a meal in my belly. People everywhere have come to my rescue when it was least expected.

One day when I was 22, I found myself hitch-hiking along the ancient Silk Road from England to India. I'd made it as far as the North Caucasus in Russia but found myself in a bit of a tight spot. My travelling companion had disappeared back home to London and there I was, alone, dealing with the aftermath of the second Chechen war. I'd managed to get detained by the Russian secret police more times than I could remember and all I wanted to do was go home myself. I'd been told I couldn't travel over the mountains for security reasons and that the only way to get to the south was on a boat across the Black Sea.

I'd stamped out of Russia in the port of Sochi, where an ill-tempered border guard had warned me, 'The Georgians are terrible people.' Her words echoed in my mind as I made my way to the stern of the little ferry to bid farewell to Russia through the haze. I was glad to have got out OK, but to be honest I was wary of the country ahead.

It wasn't long, however, before I was approached by some fellow passengers heading to the Georgian city of Poti. One of them stood out from the rest. Lasha was a tall, red-haired man, about the same age as me, who spoke broken English. He asked where I was going.

I told him I was on a journey to India, which left him looking rather blank.

'But are you looking forward to Georgia?' he asked me excitedly.

I didn't want to tell him that I wasn't too sure actually. In Russia I'd been arrested and questioned on suspicion of being a Chechen terrorist on numerous occasions and I was feeling on edge. Besides, if you believed everything on the news then the region was ablaze: Islamic insurgents hiding on every hill, bombs going off in the cities and bandits galore causing trouble in the villages. It made me think twice about talking to strangers.

'Of course,' I told him, deciding to keep my preconceptions to myself.

At that he gave me a beaming smile and slapped me on the back like an old friend. 'Then you will be my honoured guest and you must stay in my home. You will love it there and you will be my good friend.'

Swept up in his warm demeanour and his genuine offer of friendship, I relished the thought of getting to know him and of staying in a family home. Georgia had not left me lonely for long. We disembarked from the boat and walked through Poti as Lasha told me about his family. 'After the Cold War we had to flee our homes and now my family are divided. Some of them are stuck in Russia – who knows if they're dead or alive. And we are now here, refugees in someone else's city.' Poti was crumbling, and piles of garbage covered the pavements.

I was welcomed into Lasha's home with open arms and though I could see that life was tough in Poti – no one I met had electricity or running water – everywhere I went I was lavished with coffee, home brew and cakes. That evening Lasha's cousin played beautifully on the piano and we sang and danced late into the night and they showered me with gifts of chocolate and sweets. That night I lay on Lasha's living-room floor listening to the rain, grateful to him that I wasn't sleeping rough that night as I had done a lot on my journey. Life here was simple but I hadn't heard anyone complain. They smiled widely and their hospitality was boundless. The families stuck together and looked after not only each other, but anyone passing through who happened to be in need.

Lasha had changed many of my presumptions about his homeland. A place that I'd thought of as faraway and different, yet what I discovered were people not too different from my own; I'd feared Georgia might be hostile, but it turned out to be home to one of the kindest families I'd met. I thought back to the border guard's xenophobic caution and wondered how fear and prejudice could bore so deep into a person's beliefs. I've travelled in all sorts of guises – backpacker, photographer, explorer, writer, and as a soldier. In the army you're trained to be cautious and suspicious – analysing the potential threat that any stranger might have. But for me, travel was my first love and I like to think it gave me a grounding in being open. Very few people are really out to cause harm and the news reports only tell one side of the story.

When walking or hitch-hiking you're forced to interact and play the part of the guest. I've learned that you are at the mercy of the kindness of strangers the whole time. A traveller must rely on other people, trusting in the advice and hospitality of locals. Of course one must use common sense and instincts to stay safe, but in my experience the times I'd shown most vulnerability, I'd been met with nothing but respect and kindness. When you open up your mind and your soul, then and only then can you find common ground. For me travel has always been about breaking down boundaries and looking for what unites us. This book is a celebration of those people who challenge the prevailing myths, stereotypes and lazy narratives we so often see in the media. These stories show that the world is indeed a decent place and more things bring us together than set us apart.

In the end I spent a week with Lasha and his family. They fed me like a prince, even though they were struggling to make ends meet. Everything was shared. I left with a rucksack full of food, a decent bottle of wine and a bus fare to my next destination – they'd insisted on nothing less.

INTRODUCTION

Fearghal O'Nuallain

ran, on the outskirts of Tabriz, a cold evening in early December 2009.

'Follow me,' said the man with the frown. 'Is too cold for outside tonight.'

Without a thought I was chasing the dim red tail lights of a Peugeot 306 along a dark country road on my bike.

The man was dressed in a fancy suit and must have been on his way to an important gathering. A small boy, also dressed in a shiny suit, had pointed from the passenger's seat as I studied my map by the light of the petrol station. It was below freezing and I had really hoped I wouldn't have to camp in my two-season sleeping bag.

I followed the car for almost an hour, him stopping every few minutes for me to catch up, then driving off with a belch of smoke and a rattling exhaust. Eventually we arrived at an empty warehouse. The man lit the stove, and the boy fetched water for tea and made a bed in the guard house. Then they disappeared in a hurry. The man returned later with kebabs, water, biscuits and a crisp 100,000 rial note. 'Khomeini... for luck...' he said with a wink before patting my shoulder and disappearing into the night. I warmed my hands and dried my wet clothes on the stove and admired the note. It had an imposing picture of Ayatollah Khomeini on the front and something written in elegant Farsi penmanship. On the reverse was a sketch of an impressive mausoleum backed by fir trees. Next to it I was surprised to find a line written in English: 'Human beings are members of a whole. In creation of one essence and soul.' As I drifted to sleep next to the warm stove I chewed on the sentiment in my head like a toffee; one essence and soul... members of a whole...

The fire had gone out when I awoke shivering at dawn. I packed hastily and rolled my bike out onto the quiet icy road. The man hadn't told me his name, he had just given me a hot meal and somewhere warm to sleep.

A few months ago I found the note tucked into a journal. I googled the quote. It was from a poem by Saadi, an Iranian poet who lived in the thirteenth century. It was from his masterpiece, 'Gulistan', or 'The Rose Garden', Wikipedia told me. Gulistan is 'poetry of ideas with mathematical concision', it said, possibly the most influential piece of Persian literature ever written. I read on and came across the following lines:

If one member is afflicted with pain,
other members uneasy will remain.
If you have no sympathy for human pain,
the name of human you cannot retain.

That's the essence of *The Kindness of Strangers*. This is a book for humans – for people who cannot sit easily when others are afflicted. People who recognise that irrespective of the colour of our passport, the language we speak or the god we pray to, we are members of something bigger than our immediate tribe.

Our organisation, Kindness of Strangers, has a simple aim: use the power of storytelling to build empathy with people from other places. We aim to tell stories that make your heart grow. It was co-founded by Dan Martin, Rayleen Hillman and me in September 2015. Both Dan and I had been to visit the camp in Calais, known as the 'Jungle'. We found a shanty like the ones we'd encountered in Asia, Africa and South America, and it was full of people. Spirited people who'd travelled long distances and endured unimaginable hardships. We were ashamed that they were being subjected to such squalid living conditions in what we considered our part of the world. Around the world, Europe is held as a shining beacon of civilisation and fairness, and yet here were vulnerable people being left to rot. Having received such kindness when we were cold and hungry, we felt guilty that we were not doing something to help.

Winter was coming, so we asked the adventure community to help. Adventure is in the Kindness of Strangers' DNA. Adventurous travel takes us places and connects us to people we wouldn't otherwise meet; the mix of risk, challenge and uncertainty is an experience that changes people for the better. So we knew they wouldn't let us down. Two weeks later we had standing-room only at our first storytelling event, and collected enough gear to fill a transit van. Dan drove the van to Calais that night and then ended up spending the next two years working in refugee camps across Europe.

They say that travel broadens the mind, but travel also opens the heart. It's impossible to experience the world and not come home with greater empathy and concern for it. These are stories told by people who have undertaken amazing journeys and achieved impressive feats, but the tales in these pages are not of their achievements; they are stories of the charity they received, grateful elegies to the simple acts of the kindness that made their journeys possible. Our brave adventurers were aided on their quests by kind strangers who were uneasy seeing others in distress and discomfort.

This is a book for people with heart; people who recognise that kindness is the human trait that connects us with the rest of the world, and understand that it transcends the sometimes nasty narratives of history and politics. The stories in this book show that its force is strong in all corners of the world, and that it can be called upon in jungles, deserts, mountains, slums and the green fields of England. This book is an antidote to the darkness and ignorance of our times. It is a book for those of an open mind and heart, and an adventurous spirit.

This book, published in England in 2018, echoes the words written 700 years ago by an Iranian poet and printed today on the back of 100,000 rial notes. Words that we should not forget.

*Human beings are members of a whole,
in creation of one essence and soul.*

01
LET US DRINK TEA

Good people, kind people,
funny people, mad and sad
and one or two bad people

Alastair Humphreys

> *'I wonder how many people I've looked at all my life and never seen.'*
>
> **John Steinbeck, *The Winter of Discontent***

The people I meet are a highlight of the journey. I meet good people, kind people, funny people, mad and sad and one or two bad people. But mostly it is a random selection of good people. Many invite me to their homes for chai, for food or to spend the night.

One day a stylish man stops his motorbike to chat for a few minutes. His hair is swept back; he has a big bushy beard and a smear of red paste on his forehead. He wears three gold rings and a chunky gold necklace. His pretty wife and daughter are perched on the back of the bike. They are sharing the headphones of an iPod Shuffle. He tells me he works in a bank. He hands me his business card.

'Come and drink tea when you reach my town!' he calls as the family hoot, wave and roar away.

I take up the invitation. The bank is the first air-conditioned building I have been into in India. I am aware of how dirty I am. I find my new friend at a computer, data-entering a pile of cheques. My shoes stink. He smiles in welcome, shakes my hand and slaps me on the shoulder.

'Let us drink tea.'

I want to ask some of the questions I've been unable to answer walking through areas where nobody spoke much English. About rural poverty and India's rising power, about the caste system, inequality and water wars. But he is not interested in any of that. He only wants to know about England. It's good to be reminded that my normal life, my normal home and normal country are as interesting as anywhere else when seen with fresh and open eyes. The barrage of questions is charmingly frank.

'Are you having love marriages or arranged marriages? If your father does not like your girl will he ban you from his home? Are you circumcised? How many castes are there in England? Are you Christian? Are English villages like Indian villages? Do villages have water and electricity as well as the towns? Does it really rain every day?'

I still have not seen an angry person. Indians seem to share the same mild characteristics as their revered cows. But one day I see an Indian cry. The sight jolts me. A middle-aged man, his spectacles askew, a friend's arm round his shoulder, pushes through the market crowd. His eyes are shiny and numb with grief. Surrounded by the noise and rush of so many strangers it is easy to forget that each has an individual story.

Most of my memories of people are from the briefest of connections. Moments that flash through the gulfs between our lives and simply connect on a human level. A woman, about my age, is running down the road towards me. She is wearing a red and orange sari. It is rare to see Indians running, particularly women. I like the way her gold bracelets jangle and the self-conscious look on her face as she runs. I smile. She catches my smile, grins back at me, but keeps running. Two people on the same road at the same time. Our lives meet, but in opposite directions, and then we pass out of each other's lives for ever.

ABOUT ALASTAIR

Alastair Humphreys is a British adventurer and author. He has been on expeditions all around the world, travelling through over 80 countries by bicycle, boat and on foot.

———

Find out more about Alastair at:

W: www.alastairhumphreys.com ✦ T: @Al_Humphreys

I: @al_humphreys ✦ F: Alastair Humphreys ✦ P: @al_humphreys

02

STOP GIVING AND START TAKING

The importance of taking
tea in the Calais 'Jungle'

Amelia Burr

'I was an epidemiologist in Sudan,' said Dr Hammady casually in the Sunday sunshine. We sat outside his wooden shack on white plastic patio chairs in the dust of the Calais Jungle. I had taken food parcels to his community every week for months but this was the first time I'd stopped for tea. In the mania of delivering basic food rations to thousands of people, these moments took me by surprise. Load the van, drop off food, reload the van and repeat without appearing to be in a callous rush. Go, go, go. And then stop. A few words stopped me in my tracks and hit me with a stark reality.

It's not surprising that a refugee would be a doctor or a professor, although this is not the image of 'victim' we are sold in the media. In that moment, though, I was struck by the sheer waste of life in that place. This man had saved countless lives in his work. With his knowledge and skill he had prevented thousands upon thousands of deaths and here he was, waiting for me to arrive with a delivery of kidney beans and rice. His beaming smile and boundless good cheer compounded my awareness of the injustice which was alive and kicking in my act of giving. As I handed boxes down to him out of the back of the van, I thought, *This man is not my equal – he is my superior.* I'd never demonstrated the courage and aptitude needed to make the journey he had, but most of all, he had used the gift of his mind to make the world a tangibly better place.

What a ludicrous situation that this brilliant doctor should be dependent on me for such simple offerings.

Every time I saw Dr Hammady he was gracious and grateful for our work. 'Sometimes I imagine you are angels coming from the sky to lend a hand to us,' he said with his hands cast to the heavens. Smartly turned out in what appeared to be a crisply ironed Tesco employee shirt, he thanked God for the volunteers, prayed for us and even offered to go on camera to visiting journalists to help raise money to support our efforts. Like so many Sudanese in the camp, being able to cook and eat together in his community made a huge difference to him because sharing food is a cornerstone of his culture. When a Sudanese man stole from a kitchen providing free food in the Jungle, the community he lived with punished him by making him eat alone for two weeks.

Food is a simple thing to give because everybody needs it. My friend Tina Brocklebank and I set up a system where we would visit every dwelling in the camp once a week with a stamped Post-it note food ticket for every home marked with the number of people who lived there, which could be exchanged for a week's worth of food rations and firewood at the various vans parked nearby. We didn't have to agonise over who 'deserved' our help the most, because everyone needs to eat. Those days walking around the maze-like shanty town in the sunshine, wind and rain seem like a distant dream now. With the frenzy of raising enough money to feed 10,000 people going on 'backstage' at the warehouse, this was the live performance. Driving off the motorway of an industrial port town in northern France, we would go through a checkpoint manned by the bulldogs of the French police – the CRS. Then the jigsaw Jungle came into view, a mosaic of the unwanted huddled around fires, playing cricket in the road, shouting welcomes in different languages with outstretched arms and wide smiles. At every turn down the makeshift roads, lined with shacks covered in different-coloured tarpaulin, we would meet another joker. They would stand in front of the van and fold their arms, reclining on the bonnet before shooting us a cheeky smile and coming to the window for a chat. We were engulfed in the life force of this world within a world. We stepped inside people's homes to give them their food ticket. Blankets stapled to the walls for warmth and beauty, flags and photographs on display, 10,000 offers of tea and food. We were let in. We were shown kindness. This way of doing things was a big step up from the line distributions out of the back of a van which preceded it, encouraging hundreds of the most able-bodied camp residents to enter a dehumanising scrum for a measly bag of tinned food. But it still held within it the power of giving because we had to ascertain how many people lived in each shelter to give the appropriate amount of food. This number was usually a lot less than that given by the occupants. A typical interaction would be a cheerful hello in Arabic or Pashto, a comedic attempt at small talk in said language, and then the question 'How many people live here?' Let the games begin! Afghan tents with three beds inside would shout '*Pinzalas*' in cheeky unison – that's 15 in Pashto. Sudanese tents with ten beds inside would say '*Hamsa wa ishreen*' – 25 in Arabic. Laughing and lightly joking all the way, we would tactfully negotiate down to a more realistic number. They knew and we knew they were exaggerating the numbers but we also knew the amount of food we gave would not realistically last a week, so usually we met somewhere in the middle. But we had the final say and there lay the power. The only power *they* had was to refuse our ticket altogether, which some did in dramatic fashion, but for many this wasn't an option because they needed the food and wood. Receiving help, especially when you have little option to refuse it, is a powerless and humiliating position to be in. What can, to the untrained eye, seem like an uncomplicated act of kindness – to go to a refugee camp on a proverbial white horse and GIVE – can be received in a variety of different ways. Some people, like Dr Hammady, were truly grateful, seeing the desired intention – to offer a little independence and a glimmer of humanity in the forgotten darkness.

Some proud men refused our help with disdain, the humiliation of the handout not deemed worth the 'prize' on offer. Others were indifferent, or took the opportunity to milk everything they could from 'bleeding heart' volunteers – an offer of a food parcel could easily turn into a shopping list: 'I need a phone, size forty-two shoes, some tarpaulin and do you have any moong beans?'

The majority of people I met in the Jungle were either embarrassingly grateful or indifferent. The only violent reaction we experienced was borne out of the humiliation inherent in the act of giving and showed me how our 'kindness' could be perceived.

After finishing one round of food distribution we were driving out of the Jungle to go and reload the van for round two. It would often take quite a while to get out of the camp as one person after another would stop the van just to chat or to ask for something. We had already been half an hour bunny-hopping down the 'high street' when we stopped outside Khan's caravan.

This thoroughfare was the hub of the Jungle, a bustling row of makeshift shops and restaurants with the smell of fresh bread and Jungle delicacies, such as Afghan spicy eggs, wafting out of doorways. Men huddled round phone charging points, drinking tea and watching Bollywood films on big TV screens. Mountains of cigarettes wrapped up in tinfoil cylinders of ten for one euro and the latest in Afghan Jungle fashion hanging from the windows. At night this place transformed into the 'black market' – not somewhere to go alone. If you had your phone stolen, this was where your friends in the camp would go to see if they could buy it back. Shoes from our warehouse were big business on the black market – a depressing sight for new volunteers, who earnestly believed that that man really did desperately need those trainers, but most became philosophical in the end about the Jungle economy. As long as the people who desperately need shoes have them, who cares what systems evolve to swap one thing for another? That was a 'free market economy' if ever I saw one.

Khan was a businessman in the Jungle. Who knows what brought him there, but he stayed to make money. He ran a restaurant and had his fingers in multiple pies. On six days out of seven he was as sweet as the milk tea he made for us, but he could snap when the largely ignored power dynamic between camp residents and volunteers became visible through disagreements or decisions made by volunteers which would affect camp residents. Most volunteers in Calais were young, white, British women. Around 95 per cent of camp residents were men, from Sudan, Afghanistan, Eritrea, Ethiopia, Iraq, Iran and Syria. For an older Afghan man, the very idea of receiving help from a younger white woman was humiliating in and of itself.

Khan had threatened to smash up our van a few times with a confusing array of accusations about not taking him food or not going to his home at the right time. We'd tried to resolve the situation, but this was all just a dance around the real issue – the helping. There is no right way to help a man who feels belittled by the very intention. As we began to chat to someone out of the window of our van, he suddenly flew out of his caravan with a hammer and started smashing the windscreen. Glass was coming in at us on the front seat as he kept hammering and shouting. After a few minutes he stopped and we left unharmed, but his uncontrollable anger left its mark. In 14 months of being in the Jungle nearly every day, that was the only time I felt unsafe. We were always surrounded by people who took pride in looking after us. I was shown more kindness in the camp than in any other place I have ever been. But that day I realised what our 'kindness' meant to some people. It made them feel small and, let's face it, emasculated.

For our part we did what we could to minimise the indignity of giving through the ticket system, but what made the most difference was making time to be the receiver. Taking tea in someone's home or letting them cook you dinner created an all-important exchange. Those times when I received kindness from strangers were truly the most powerful, soul-filling moments of my life. To be lavished with generosity by people who had next to nothing was humbling for me and made my hosts grow two inches taller. It allowed friendship to blossom on an even plane. There were pockets of sanctuary dotted all over the Jungle – the places I could go for five minutes out of the madness, for peace, a kind word, a cup of tea and a breath of air, for the 'me' behind my smile. I have cried on a friend in his humble home by a rat-infested river and I have received his tears when his two sisters in Sudan both died of cancer within a month. I have danced in the night rain at my thirty-fifth birthday party surrounded by music played by talented musicians, serenaded with poetry written for me, enveloped in love from my fellow humans. I've been given a pair of new boots when my old ones were falling off my feet and I have enjoyed the best hot dinners of all my days.

Because we received we were allowed to give in a way that would be taken as a favour from one friend to another. Before the camp was demolished I realised that the food was just a ruse, a way for us to come to the table with something. Infinitely more valuable was what our hosts then put on the table for us, with a sense of dignity and pride. Our greatest gift was to receive kindness from strangers.

To receive is vital to the act of giving. Otherwise, you are, in fact, taking something away.

ABOUT AMELIA

Amelia Burr was a local newspaper reporter in London before she quit to volunteer in Calais for 14 months. There, she co-managed the delivery of food parcels to every dwelling in what was the largest shanty town in Europe. She recently returned to the UK to live in the woods near Bristol. Amelia remains committed to volunteering in the refugee crisis... once she has enjoyed a brief period of digging holes and chopping wood in solitude.

03
THE WEICHMAN SISTERS

When an attempt to out-cycle a blizzard doesn't quite go to plan

Anna McNuff

The cold October day I met the Weichman family was the worst I'd had in three months on the road. A relentless South Dakotan crosswind had nudged me back and forth for 80 miles, and in the midst of an attempt to out-cycle a blizzard which was tracking its way across the USA, I'd been riding for almost two weeks without a break. By the time I rolled into the tiny town of Bison, population 342, I was in a real slump.

Pedalling into town, my mind was focused on two things, and two things alone: sleep and food. For the past three months I'd spent most nights in my tent. Today I'd decided that I would really push the boat out and treat myself to a night at the motel in town. I mean that literally – it really was the only motel in town. The plan was to get a good night's kip, and an early start the following day.

Bison wasn't much larger in real life than the dot on the map. Two large cylindrical metal grain stores poked up from the landscape, and were surrounded by modest one-storey farm buildings – a sight that had become familiar in the American Midwest. I was just preparing to turn right down the 'main street' when a rusty grey estate car appeared alongside me. I'd only been passed by two cars that day and so this in itself was a monumental event. At first I kept my gaze fixed forward, waiting for the car to pass, but it seemed to be moving unusually slowly. Turning my head to the left, I looked into the car. In the driver's seat was a young girl, and she was waving – waving so enthusiastically that I feared her whole right arm might just detach and fly off into the windscreen.

I looked back to the road ahead, thinking perhaps I had imagined it, and then I looked left again. There she was – still waving, still smiling, and madly. And so I, being the dignified lady I am, responded with a wave of equal magnitude, coupled with a gigantic grin. The grin 'n' wave combo must have had an impact on the girl because a little further on in the centre of town she pulled off the road into a gravel car park and leaped swiftly from the car.

When I entered the car park myself, she was still breathless from her speedy car exit and panted excitedly: 'Where... are... you from?!'

I squeezed on the brakes and ground to a halt, dismounted my beautiful pink touring bicycle and kicked out the stand. 'Oh! I'm, um, from England,' I replied, upping my BBC British accent a little more than usual.

She clasped her hands together under her chin, balled them into a fist, smiled broadly and squealed. The kind of high-pitched squeal that only dogs might be able to hear. 'Ooook! I've never met anyone from England!' she exclaimed, her eyes ablaze. 'We don't get many visitors here. What are you doing in Bison?!'

And so we proceeded to indulge in a mutual exchange of whos, whys, whens and wheres. Her excitement was infectious, and so both of our voices became increasingly high-pitched. Imagine two overexcited puppies meeting in a park, minus the butt sniffing. During the exchange I learned that the sweet girl standing in front of me was 21-year-old Katie Weichman. She had mousy brown hair tied in a high, loose ponytail and hazel eyes, and was dressed in grey tracksuit bottoms and a pink hoodie. Katie was a shot glass full of sunshine, and the energy she exuded transfused itself into my weary veins.

'Well, you've just gotta come back to our farm. It's just up the road,' said Katie in an accent that resembled those I'd only ever heard in *Fargo*. 'You know that blizzard is due, and we'd love to have you visit with us for a few days. My sister would just love to meet you! And Auntie – oh, Auntie would adore you!' She stared at me and blinked. Her soft voice had all the innocence of a child, and her eyes were wide, like a Disney princess.

I was a little taken aback by her offer. I hadn't expected to meet anyone today, let alone be invited home for tea. Today was set to be a crap, 'get it done' kind of a day.

'Oh, that's so kind... um... Where's your farm?' I asked, thinking that 'just up the road' didn't sound like too far to cycle.

'Eleven miles back that-a-way.' She grinned and pointed over her shoulder and back in the direction I'd come from. And then she stared and blinked at me again with those eyes.

Eleven miles back? This girl was sweet, but I was really tired. I didn't fancy an extra 22-mile cycle to her home and back to here in the morning. I really needed to get some decent sleep and just get on my way.

'Oh, thank you, thanks so much, but it's OK. I'll just stay here in town. I've got to be on the road early tomorrow.'

Her expression shifted from bright and breezy to confused, and her mouth drooped a little. 'But, but – there's a blizzard coming?'

'Yeah, yeah – I'm going to try to, err... out-pedal it...' I could hear how ridiculous it sounded as the words left my mouth, but I couldn't take them back.

I could see that Katie was just about to protest some more, when a truck pulled into the car park. 'Oook, look! My brother!' she squealed. 'Come meet his kids!'

I went over and chatted for a few minutes with some of the other Weichman family, but as everyone was engaged in conversation, I took this as a chance to make a polite exit. I told Katie that it was lovely to meet her, and pedalled off down the road, following the original plan and heading for the motel.

Cycling off, I couldn't help but feel, for want of a better word, icky. Something in the pit of my stomach felt distinctly odd. What the hell was I doing? That girl had just extended to me the greatest kindness, and I had declined it for a night on my own in a motel. I didn't even like motels. They mostly smelled of boiled cabbage and came with other people's pubic hair scattered around the toilet seat. My refusal of Katie's offer felt completely wrong. I stopped to look back to the car park, and considered turning around. Katie was laughing and throwing the young blond-haired kids around in the air. I couldn't go back now – she was enjoying time with her family and I didn't want to be a burden – so I continued on and checked into the motel.

An hour later, I was surrounded by a recently exploded kit-bomb. My tent, bike tools, panniers and food were strewn all over the room. Cycling clothing dripped from every available surface like a Salvador Dalí painting. I was just removing my sleeping bag from its case to give it a good overnight airing when I heard a knocking. I dismissed it as a knock for the people in the room opposite, and turned my attention back to unpacking my musty sleeping cocoon. But there it was again, a knocking... and I could swear it was my door. I moved to the other side of the room and tentatively opened it. Standing on the other side was Katie.

'Hey! I, um... thought I'd come visit!' she chirped, holding out her arms for a hug, which I enveloped her in immediately. Her innocence was just adorable.

I ushered her inside and, sitting on beds opposite one another, we picked up our chatting where we had left off before her family arrived at the car park.

Just then her phone rang: 'Ooook, it's my sister! Hang on... Y'ello, Dorena. Uh huh... yees... mmm huh... oh, I'm just with her now...' Katie dropped the phone away from her ear and looked at me. 'Are you sure you won't come back to the farm? Dorena says she'd just love to visit with you.'

That was it – I didn't need asking twice. I nodded and Katie squealed.

'Yes! She said yes. See you soon, Dorena!'

Despite having paid for the motel room, I crammed all of my stuff back into the bags and, as I flung the key back into the hands of the bemused receptionist, yelled: 'I'm going with Katie!'

Katie threw my bike in the boot of her car, and drove me back to the family farm.

Turning off the main road at a large oak tree, we bounced down a rocky half-mile-long track. We pulled into the farm, and a single-storey blue house with white window frames came into view. It was slightly raised off the ground on stilts and there was a ramp leading up to the front door. The outside was clad in wooden slats, and in the front yard was an assortment of hay bales and a big red tractor. To the left-hand side of the house was a long, white static trailer.

'So here it is!' said Katie, turning the key to kill the car engine. 'That's our home.' She pointed to the blue house. 'I live there with Dorena and Grannie and Auntie. And that...' she pointed to the white trailer, '... that's where my brother Ethan lives. Not the one you met earlier – that was our oldest brother. Ethan is a bit younger – you'll meet him, his wife Amber and little Christopher soon. Oh, you'll love Christopher!'

'Lovely,' I said, almost to myself, already feeling glad to be here and not at the motel. 'Do your parents live here too?'

'Oh no, they live about forty-five minutes up the ways. We look after Grannie and Auntie.'

'Oh. How old are Grannie and Auntie?'

'Ooo, now, well, let me see...' Katie bit her bottom lip and stared at the floor. 'Grannie just turned eighty-eight, and Auntie... well, Auntie would be ninety-eight!'

'And you look after them – just you and Dorena?!'

Katie nodded and gave a simple, distracted 'Mmmm hmm', as if it were the most normal thing in the world. 'Oook, look! There's Dorena!'

The door to the blue house was now open and a young woman was standing in the doorway. It had started to get dark so Dorena was lit by a soft orange glow coming from the kitchen behind her. She waved almost as enthusiastically as her younger sister had done earlier that afternoon, and I waved right back.

Sitting inside at the kitchen table, with a girl I'd known for only three hours, and her older sister for even less, I felt strangely at home. It was gone 8 p.m., but Dorena insisted on cooking up a feast for us all. I troughed down pizza, hot chocolate, marshmallows and ice cream, as we three chatted into the wee hours: about religion, family, boys and life growing up in small-town Bison. Twenty-seven-year-old Dorena, who had all the kindness of her little sister but the air of a mother goose about her, made it very clear that I could stay with them just as long as I wanted to. And at last I relented. My trip schedule was no match for the hearts of these two. Regardless of whether the blizzard hit tomorrow, I decided that I would spend the following day getting to know the Weichman sisters a little better. There was a magic about them and their home that filled a void. It nourished me from the inside out. After 92 days of cycling alone, I craved attention, company and genuine affection, and this family was offering it all.

I was up at 6.30 a.m. the following morning and ambled bleary-eyed into the kitchen to find Dorena humming and busying herself, chopping fruit and stirring oatmeal on the stove. She spotted me in the hallway and lit up.

'Morning!' she cooed, immediately coming over to give me a hug. 'How did you sleep?'

'Like a baby,' I replied, emerging from her monster embrace, and it was true. I'd passed out before my head had hit the pillow and woken up dehydrated, without a clue of where I was.

According to the latest local forecast, snow wasn't due until later in the day, and so we had all agreed that there was more than enough time for me to make a trip into town to talk to kids at the local school about my bike ride through the 50 states. I said I'd pick up some supplies while in town (it was the least I could do) and the Weichman sisters kindly offered the use of their car, which I accepted. After the obligatory turning on of the headlights instead of windscreen wipers (high beam, of course), over-revving the engine and trying to drive off with the car in 'park' mode, I eventually got on my way. I dropped into the school for an hour and chatted to the eleventh-grade kids. They were aloof at first, as teenagers tend to be, but eventually I used the two most powerful tools at my disposal to break down the barriers: a strong British accent and disgusting amounts of energy and enthusiasm. Once they opened up, there was the usual, although notably more mature, barrage of questions, plus a few specials, like, 'Do you know Bear Grylls?' I explained, not personally, no, and they went on to ask: 'Didn't he row down the River Thames? Naked in a bathtub?' I couldn't be sure if this was one of his accomplishments.

When I emerged from the school at 10 a.m., the kids were being sent home early because the blizzard had started and the skies were already putting in a big snow-shift. I made my way over to the grocery store to pick up some supplies for the ranch, just as Dorena 'big sis' Weichman called. She was concerned about me making it the 11 miles home safely in the snow, but I assured her that I would drive slowly. She offered some last-ditch advice: 'If you start to slide, don't brake, just slide, OK?' Yikes. I loaded up the car with the food and began the drive back at 20 mph, much to the despair of other motorists, thundering along behind me in their sensible big-tyre trucks.

All was going well (ish) on the drive home. I was starting to lose visibility out of the windscreen, but that didn't matter because I was almost at the big oak tree and the turn-off to the ranch. As it happens, trying to find an unmarked dirt road off a highway when everything is covered in white isn't easy. I was lacking in spidey sense and I missed it. Five minutes later, my spidey sense kicked in, and I knew I'd gone too far. I proceeded to accost and converse with a plethora of other passing road users, including a busload of schoolkids, who seemed to find my plight rather entertaining. Despite explaining that I was staying with the Weichmans, no one could accurately describe where I needed to be, largely because I had no idea where that was, and of course to make matters worse, my phone battery had now died and I couldn't call Dorena, who would no doubt be worried about me by now.

I flagged down another passing truck and asked the teenagers inside if I could use their phone, before realising that I didn't know what number to call. So instead I followed them slowly in the car to their grandma's house. Their grandma knew the Weichmans, and she called them for me. They explained to her the location of the ranch, in relation to where I currently was, which was, of course, nowhere near where I had started.

The grandma and young boys started to give me directions to drive back to the ranch, but I was well and truly done. In the hour since flagging them down, the snow had thickened just that bit past sensible (when was this ever sensible?), and there was no way I was getting back behind the wheel. So instead I abandoned the car and accepted a ride home from two 14-year-old boys (it's legal to drive from 14 in South Dakota). Shopping intact, but with my dignity in tatters, I made it 'home' to the ranch. By the time I walked through the door, it seemed the whole Bison community knew there was a girl from London lost in the snow. The parents of the family had been called, as had the sister, and the older brother was now out looking for me.

As it turned out, the blizzard I was trying to out-pedal was a record-breaker. Four feet of snow fell in just 24 hours and I watched from the living-room window that afternoon as the world around me slowly turned completely white. Through a mixture of visits from icicle-encrusted neighbours, calls and texts, we learned that the blizzard had left 22,000 people across the state without power. There were now only two houses in the town of Bison that still had power, and I was sitting in one of them.

An impending power cut was something that really worried the girls. Dorena told me that Auntie relied on an oxygen machine to help her breathe – if they lost power, they would hook up the emergency oxygen bottle, but that bottle would only last 24 hours. The roads were so thick with snow that making the two-hour drive to collect a new bottle was now an impossibility.

At times, when Auntie came out of her room to perch on the sofa, led by the two sisters, with her oxygen machine trailing behind, I felt uneasy. Here I was, a fit and healthy middle-class Londoner, placing an added strain on a family who had a terminally ill 98-year-old to look after. I reasoned that I was providing a welcome distraction, and did my best to help out by adopting the role of babysitter-in-residence for the littlest member of the family, 18-month-old Christopher. For days I cooed, threw myself on the floor, and played peek-a-boo – all to keep him entertained.

The blizzard raged on for days, and the health of their elderly relatives wasn't the girls' only concern. The cows were the Weichmans' livelihood, and so I soon learned that keeping them safe was the top priority. A priority that I could offer little assistance with, it seemed. I, as it turned out, was as useful as a chocolate teapot. Partly because I had no idea how to look after or indeed hunt for escapologist cows, and partly because I slept for most of the first two days. My back ached, I had waves of headaches and sometimes I would be so tired in the afternoons that I'd fall asleep where I was sitting. Often it takes being forced to be still to realise just how exhausted you are. And I was exhausted.

I learned that Dorena was quite the real-life cowgirl. She would spend hours with brother Ethan and his wife Amber, chasing down the runaway cows through pastures, wading in knee-deep snow, sometimes in the dark, as Katie stayed behind to look after Auntie and Grannie. Twice Dorena and Ethan had to abandon a pickup truck or tractor in the snow and hike the five miles home. Cold, dehydrated and famished, Dorena would tumble through the door, and, following a three-minute sit-down, promptly begin cooking dinner, washing up and checking on Auntie. When she was at home, a new smell would waft from the stove every few hours: potato soup, pulled pork, roast chicken, homebaked bread, cookies. I never went hungry and not once did I see the girls stop smiling. The Weichmans' home managed to maintain power through the storm, and despite it claiming the lives of 14,000 cattle across the state, thanks to their dedication, Ethan and the girls only lost one of theirs.

On the evening of the fourth day at the ranch, I was rested but restless. The snow had stopped falling at last, and so I trudged the half mile up to the main highway to check on the state of the roads. Although the white stuff was still piled well over head height at the sides of the highway, I found what I was looking for: tarmac. The snowploughs had made it out and I now had a clear passage out of town.

The following morning, I filled up on pancakes, sausages, porridge and fruit at the breakfast table. I repacked my panniers, and threw in a small bag of homebaked cookies before turning to hug the Weichman sisters for one last time. I looked past them at the ranch, at the dogs playing out the front, and Grannie standing in the doorway. At the snow still covering every surface and little Christopher in Amber's arms. The reality was that I may never see this family again. And even if I did, it'd be years from now. I wheeled slowly away with a lump in my throat and an empty feeling in the pit of my stomach. The relief to be on the move again was coupled with deep sadness and an overwhelming sense of gratitude. They truly felt like my family now. Only a family could still accept someone who would abandon their car, eat them out of house and home, and sleep all the hours God sent. Wasn't life grand? Just when I'd needed it most, the world had thrown the Weichmans in my path.

ABOUT ANNA

Anna is an adventurer, speaker and mischief-maker. Once upon a time she represented Great Britain at rowing, but after 'retiring' in her mid-twenties, she began darting around the world on the hunt for new and exciting endurance challenges. Recently named by *The Guardian* as one of the top female adventurers of our time, she has also been placed in the 'top 50 most influential travellers in the world' by *Condé Nast Traveller*.

In 2013 she set out to ride a beautiful pink bicycle 11,000 miles through each and every state of the USA, before going on to become the first person to run New Zealand's Te Araroa trail, solo and unsupported – covering 1,911 miles on backcountry trails. More recently she embarked on a six-month cycle through South America, ascending as many peaks and passes of the Andes mountains as she could along the way.

Closer to home, she spent a month cycling across Europe directed entirely by social media, ran the length of Hadrian's Wall dressed as a Roman soldier, and ran the length of the Jurassic Coast dressed as a dinosaur. As you do.

Passionate about the positive impact that adventure and sport can have on the lives of youngsters, Anna uses her human-powered journeys as a platform to inspire and enable kids to get outside, and get exploring.

———

Find out more about Anna at:

W: www.annamcnuff.com ◆ T: @AnnaMcNuff
I: @annamcnuff ◆ F: @AMcNuff

04
A SLICE OF PARADISE

A gruelling journey –
and a very great reward

Benedict Allen

Where on this planet might we hope, briefly, to find somewhere close to paradise? On a faraway beach awash with lazy turquoise waves, perhaps. Or by a pristine lagoon lined with shading palms and low-hanging fruit. Humans have been fascinated by the notion of a work-free, pest-free habitat of loveliness ever since – well, ever since Adam and Eve were expelled from it. Surely there must be somewhere better out there – so the feeling goes – some little piece of Eden left undiscovered in a distant corner of the world.

New Guinea is not that place – or at least it wasn't to me 30 years ago when I was making my way precariously through its uncharted swamps. I was chased from one village by men with drawn bows – and when, after six months, I was invited to go through a secret initiation ceremony, it was only to discover (rather too late) that the procedure involved being force-fed and scarred all over my chest and back with bamboo blades. We were also beaten every day, four or five times a day. That ceremony was designed to make each initiate 'a man as strong as a crocodile'. It went on for six weeks.

Of course, back then I was a young man. Like anyone in their early twenties I thought I was immortal. Today, three decades on, things seem rather different – and so it was with considerable misgivings that I made the decision to return last year. The BBC security correspondent Frank

Gardner and I had got talking at a bar and he'd told me how birds of paradise had fascinated him since childhood – the astounding plumage of the males, their elaborate dances to impress potential mates. 'I suppose it's my one big regret,' he said, indicating his wheelchair. 'I'll never now get to PNG to see those birds.'

I didn't really know Frank then, nor much about birds. But I did recognise a survivor in him – shot six times in a terrorist attack in Saudi, he had been to the brink of death. Besides, here was a challenge too great to refuse: New Guinea is the world's largest tropical island, famously inaccessible, but I thought I might enlist the help of the Niowra, the Sepik River people who'd put me through that ceremony.

The BBC agreed to let him go – although there'd have to be a reconnoitre and Frank must have a medic. Nothing could be allowed to go wrong.

It did, of course. But not for Frank, at least at first. Carefully, he was deposited into a canoe, wheelchair and all, with the assistance of our especially drilled local helpers – and immediately he began scanning the skies with his binoculars.

As for our heroic explorer, he hadn't taken account of the emotional impact of his return. That first day as I stared out at the humid forest, all the horrors of 30 years before came back, surfacing as if through the black mud.

'These people offered me shelter,' I murmured to Frank as two vast dugout canoes of Niowras emerged complete with painted dancers all draped in leaves and pig tusks. 'And then gave me hell.'

Somehow making it worse, the dance party giving me this boisterous greeting were composed of my *wanbanis* – that is, those I'd gone through the nightmare initiation with. Together we'd been made into 'crocodile men'. Our bond was sacred. And now I was back in the fold.

'Welcome home!' said my adopted father Jonnie, escorting me into Kandengei village as hundreds of figures in ragged T-shirts ran along the riverbank.

This isn't my home, I thought weakly. Home was Twickenham, with three screaming kids.

But of course the fanfare was a huge honour – and soon I began recognising faces. Indeed, before long I was off with my old mates, foraging for eggs left buried in compost by jungle fowl. The truth was, though their initiation rituals were almost unbelievably brutal, the Niowras also lived in an immeasurably harsh environment – these fetid swamps were riddled with disease; I learned that a third of those that I'd undergone the ceremony with were dead. These Sepik people, then, had developed a perfect role model. The crocodile was territorial; it was tough – it endured out here.

Now Frank too was beginning to suffer in this oppressive humidity – and we'd hardly travelled anywhere yet. As we headed off through the dark waters of Chambri Lake and south into the forest interior, my companion took to having a siesta – and periodically I took to looking at his face to see how he was faring. At night he was racked with pain – the nerve endings jangled by all the man-hauling. And all the while we had the knowledge that, with Frank being confined to a wheelchair, his legs had become osteoporotic; they'd shatter if he were dropped even once.

But our skills were being honed, and Frank was now borne in a sedan chair, passed from one village to another. As we made our way over the Hunstein Range there was not one false move – not one slip in all those miles. Without exception the New

Guineans treated Frank with exquisite gentleness and respect. 'This is the route along which we carry dead bodies,' the people of Yenbeyenbe explained.

By now I was expecting to see a very different Frank. With his view through the undergrowth restricted to wherever he happened to be carried, he had every right to be exasperated – not least when seeing me nipping ahead along the path, excited that the forest was still alive and well, even after all these years.

Yet not a trace of bitterness. And as we travelled yet further inland, I found myself more and more excited. This wasn't the jungle of my youth. The dense foliage that rose up ahead was no longer oppressive; I regarded it instead with wonder. So much of the world's rainforest had been ripped out but here in New Guinea mile upon mile was laid out in an undulating canopy that was as pristine as I'd left it.

Finally, high in the Central Range, Frank too was rewarded – with the sight of the flamboyant King of Saxony bird of paradise. Exquisitely beautiful and as if forever at play in the mists, he seemed to belong to a lost time and place. The bird twirled on his high branch, displaying not in hope of some eager female but – I began to believe – instead for us. Isolated in his ethereal habitat, he seemed to speak of the unquantifiable reward that we all in life seek.

ABOUT BENEDICT

Benedict Allen is particularly known for his solo expeditions through the jungle, desert and Arctic – journeys famously achieved not with a satellite phone, GPS or any of the usual 'backup', but after months of training with a remote indigenous community. These and other ventures are depicted in his ten books – including two bestsellers – and numerous television series for the BBC and elsewhere, usually filmed without a camera crew. Few people alive have spent so long isolated and alone in so many different potentially hostile environments.

Find out more about Benedict at:

W: www.benedictallen.com ✦ T: @benedictallen

05
THE GOOD SAMARITAN

How a bottle of water
changed my world

Breifne Earley

In the dry Indian heat the wet jersey stuck uncomfortably to my back with my own sweat. I'd been on the road early, rising an hour before the sun to try to get ahead of the high midday temperatures I knew were coming. A relatively straightforward three hours in the saddle had taken me to the foothills of the Western Ghat mountains, which run the entire length of India's west coast.

Hours earlier I'd struggled to find breakfast, having to settle for a cup of tea as I just couldn't stomach the only option available for breakfast, which looked as if it had been served to Oliver Twist in a former life. I was beginning to regret my choices now as I struggled to keep my energy levels high enough to stay upright on both wheels of my bike.

Eight weeks earlier I'd left my home in the north-west of Ireland with the intention of cycling around the world, and entered the World Cycle Race. Now, after injury, visa issues and a disqualification had claimed my competitors, I was the only remaining rider in the race, the most unlikely leader of a bicycle race ever seen. I knew that all I had to do was stay in the saddle, observe the rules of the race and eventually when I circumnavigated the entire globe and returned to London I would be the winner of the longest sporting event on the entire planet.

As I stared up the road ahead of me, into the mountain pass which would eventually lead me to Bangalore, almost a kilometre above sea level, I could only think of the reasons why this was crazy. I wasn't an athlete, I had only been cycling a few years and had never been part of a cycle race before. I didn't speak any of the local languages, I wasn't able to cope with the midday heat and the climbs were unlike anything I'd ever seen before – higher than anything I'd conquered in training, double the height of any road in Ireland.

As the time on my Garmin device kept ticking ever closer to noon, the temperature display just kept rising. Past 30°C and then on into the forties. My mind was racing, thinking about the consequences of turning around. I knew the cool air-conditioned room and comfortable bed I'd left at 5.30 that morning was still there at the base of the mountain, some 30 kilometres downhill. Downhill – I wouldn't even have to pedal the bike, no effort would be required; I'd simply just have to turn around and allow gravity to apologise for what it had put my legs through already that morning.

My food and water supplies were long gone and now my body was overheating and starting to rebel against my mind. I allowed my mind to wander further west, back to my home town, where 'Sure I got all the way to India!' might suffice as a response to anyone who mentioned my attempt to cycle around the world. 'It's further than any of you expected I'd get! I was the last man standing in the race – sure I might as well have won the race.' Just a day's ride further back, past that cool motel room was the airport in Mangalore, where sure I'd be able to go home and still save face with my friends, family and neighbours – anything that got me out of this heat, the sun and these damn mountains.

I had no idea where my next refuelling spot might be. The maps I was using showed no town for another 20 miles and a lot more vertical distance to cover. The regular shanties selling water and snacks on the side of the road had become a thing of the past, not having seen one in over four hours since just after daybreak. But despite the appeal of turning round and heading back to comfort and familiarity, something inside me made me push on. The heat and low energy levels finally got to me, though, and I was resigned to pushing the bike ahead of me as I trudged up the hill when the miracle happened.

A silver car passed me before its brake lights flashed and it pulled on to the hard shoulder just before the next bend in the road. A man stepped out of the driver side and stared back at me. Eventually, as I edged closer to the car, he made his way back down the road towards me. 'You look like you need some help. How can I help you?' he asked.

'I need some water. Food would be amazing.'

'If you jump in, I'll bring you to the next town,' the man immediately replied.

Immediately I was elated – the torture was going to be over – but my next thought was the rules of the race. Lee, the original leader of the race, had been eliminated because he'd taken a private car in a similar situation in India just a few weeks earlier and I knew if I jumped in the car I'd also face the same result, and all my work and effort so far would be for nothing. 'I can't,' I heard myself saying to my potential Good Samaritan, Arvind.

His confused face brought the story pouring out of me, about the race, the rules, the problems I'd have if I took assistance from anyone. His confusion turned to concern and he told me he might have some supplies in his car. When Arvind returned from his car he carried a bag of snacks and a litre bottle of water. The water was consumed in seconds and I started tucking into the snacks as if I hadn't seen food in weeks.

Arvind returned to his car for a second time and produced another bottle of water. This one made its way into my water bottles, before the remainder was tipped into my mouth. We stood in the blazing sun on the side of the road as it snaked up into the mountains. Arvind, a keen cyclist himself, was on his way home to Bangalore after a holiday with his wife (who was waiting in the car) on the west coast. We discussed my journey and I thanked him repeatedly for stopping to assist me in my moment of need.

Once I started getting back to relative normality, he waved goodbye, returned to his wife and disappeared off up the hill. I was more than a little envious of the engine that propelled the car up the mountain pass as my attention returned to my bike. The conditions were so tough that I could already feel my body heating up again and I hadn't even started cycling. I swung a leg over my crossbar, pushed off and started pushing the pedals again. As I rounded a bend a small building came into view on the other side of the road. It had what appeared to be a beer sign hanging outside, although it looked more or less deserted from a distance.

As I edged the couple of hundred metres towards the structure it became more and more obvious that this was actually a bar, with the customary hanging packets of snacks and potato crisps and fridges full of drinks sitting near the front door, plus a handful of chickens and other farm animals ambling around outside. The power came back into my legs and the last few pedal strokes seemed easy. I jumped off the bike and made my way inside the building.

There was no one there. No one to pay for what I intended to consume. I started just taking the food from the shelves, trying to raise my energy levels. I needed sugar and salt in my body after sweating all the minerals out of my system all day in the saddle.

Eventually the bar owner appeared, and produced a menu. He spoke no English so we communicated through gestures, me indicating the items I had already consumed and him disappearing and then reappearing with plates piled high with chicken. I had both lunch and dinner in my three-hour sojourn at that roadside bar, staying out of the sun until I was strong enough to continue on my adventure, before paying the huge sum of £3 for everything I'd eaten. An adventure which would eventually wind through 27 countries and 18,000 miles, before I made it back to London to be crowned as the race winner.

The only time I actually considered quitting was this day in India. Faced with every possible reason why it was too difficult, too challenging to continue onwards towards my goal, the selfless support of a complete stranger on the side of the road kept me moving forward in the right direction.

The reality is that having completed 99 per cent of the work required to get to the next fuel stop on the most challenging day of my entire journey, I was considering throwing in the towel on the entire project for a few hundred metres' more cycling. I'll never forget Arvind and the contribution that a bottle of water or two made to what has become a life-defining event for me.

This encounter played out so often across the entire world, regardless of race, gender, religion or social standing. I met generosity at almost every stage of my journey. Accommodation, lunches, drinks and company were forthcoming from perfect strangers as they offered assistance to another human being just because they were in a position to help. They form my greatest memories from the entire cycle, and years later I'm still in regular contact with so many of the people who offered help and assistance on my adventure on two wheels around the entire planet.

ABOUT BREIFNE

In late 2010, struggling with depression, Breifne Earley made the decision to end his own life, but was stopped in his tracks by a fortuitous text message. Eight years later he had completely turned his life around.

He started by setting himself a bucket list of ten personal challenges to complete between 10/10/2010 and 11/11/2011, which included starting to run and cycle, learning to swim and cook, overcoming fears, changing careers and going on 50 blind dates. He went on to complete triathlons, road races, a marathon and open-water sea swims as well as cycling around New Zealand.

Between 2014 and 2015, he spent 16 months cycling 30,000 kilometres through 27 countries to compete in and eventually win the longest sporting endurance event in the world, the World Cycle Race.

Breifne has also written and published a bestselling, award-winning book, *Pedal the Planet*, which details his story and showcases an inspiring and positive message about suicide prevention and dealing with depression.

Find out more about Breifne at:

W: www.breifneearley.com ◆ T: @BreifneEarley
I: @breifneearley ◆ F: @breifneearley

06
MAMA ANA

One summer in a
Romanian orphanage

Charlie Carroll

In the village's only bar, when the men spoke of Mama Ana, they did so quietly, glancing about and behind themselves first, as if she might be listening nearby.

'She whips their bare legs with stinging nettles.'

'No heart... no love...'

'She sharpens her teeth and her elbows.'

'Bozzy. Damn bozzy...'

The children seemed to share the opinion. They spoke no English, but their behaviour communicated volumes. Whispers rippled along the corridors or across the playground – Mama Ana... Mama Ana... Mama Ana – to signify her approach, and the yowling and the fighting and sometimes even the comfort-rocking would stop, slow, quieten. Then she would appear, being sure to look at each of them directly, steadily, once each: a tough job for there were hundreds. Few looked back. In my experience, you caught Mama Ana's eye only by mistake, and you never held it.

Cristina, the second nurse, favoured diplomacy in her descriptions. 'Yes, Mama Ana is formidable. But here we need this, no?'

'I've heard she is cruel. To the children. She uses stinging nettles and thorns as punishment, threatens them with snakes and spiders from the fields. Withholds food or water, or lets them bathe in their own excrement.'

Cristina shook her head. 'We need Mama Ana. We all do.'

'Not me,' I replied. 'I don't need her.' I was cocky. Self-righteous. Seventeen years old. And incorrect.

I fell ill early in the third week. The ever-present filth and germs which dominated the orphanage had latched on to each of us, and I was the latest in line to fall victim. My symptoms matched those of my companions before me – the sweating, the semi-delirium, the excruciating stomach cramps – and my remedy did too. I was moved from the campsite and into the orphanage itself, and given the 'sickbay': a bare room on the top floor with a bed and toilet and no windows. Consciousness was fleeting during that first day. When it came it was often accompanied by dizzying, sickening panic. But in the rare moments of clear-headedness I cursed my stupidity. I had not, I remembered, washed my hands before eating the previous day. I should have known better.

My work at the orphanage had been an education, and not just in relation to hygiene. Before my arrival, I knew little about Romania – could barely place it on a map. I had never heard of Nicolae Ceauşescu, had no idea that he had been executed for his cruel reign just eight years earlier. And I had no idea why the orphanages in Romania were so notorious, why other people nodded with faint but knowing recognition whenever I mentioned them, as if I had said 'Ethiopian famine' or 'Siberian prison'. I did not know about the appalling conditions, of how children had been abandoned in these orphanages under Ceauşescu's regime; and I did not know that now, in 1997, while the rest of Romania was free, the children were still not, that they remained institutionalised, unwanted, to all intents and purposes imprisoned.

I found out, of course. I found out on my first day there.

The orphanage I and a dozen other volunteering aid workers had been allocated to was situated in the north-west of Romania, in a small village ringed by green mountains. While the village huddled around the low river, its school and bar and shops and houses always busy and glowing with life, the orphanage sat far out from the hub, surrounded by ten-foot-high fencing, alone, quiet and ignored. It was an enormous and austere building; grey facades and brutalist right angles. Opposite the orphanage was a patch of wasteland where we set up our camp. It smelled of sun-dried urine.

Cristina welcomed us that first morning, appearing from the orphanage gates and crossing the road to our makeshift campsite, where she introduced herself to each of us in turn. 'So. Are you ready? We will let the kids out soon.'

'Out?'

'Out of the building. Into the playground. They are not allowed out of the compound.'

'Compound' was an apt word. The fence, topped with barbed wire, had but one opening: two imposing gates kept locked at all times. Cristina and Mama Ana were the only staff at the orphanage, taking care of hundreds of children between them, and one of them would let us in each morning and let us out again each evening, always locking the gates behind us. Escape, it seemed, was impossible.

'Where's the playground?' I asked as we stepped through into the compound. Before us was the orphanage, the centrepiece to an acre of dusty, potholed concrete.

'You are standing in it,' Cristina replied. 'Wait here. I will let them out.'

She walked across the playground, climbed the steps to the orphanage's front door, and opened it. A tidal wave of children spilled out. Loud and tiny, arms waving above their heads and mouths wide, they sprinted towards us, each zeroing in on their target. We were swamped in seconds. One wrapped herself around my leg while another spun me into a bear hug and a third gleefully rugby-tackled me to the ground. More joined in the pile-on. I looked across the potholes to my fellow volunteers. Each had been floored, children laughing and jumping up and down upon them like trampolines. It was overwhelming, but it was never sinister. The children were playing, the only way they knew how. And, after a lifetime of malnutrition, they weighed nothing.

We stayed with them all day. They were impossible to tire. Playing, playing, playing – it was all they wanted. They would not leave us alone, could not take their eyes off us. Each of us volunteers had been brought here because we were musicians. The idea was for us to play for the orphans. 'Musical therapy' was the phrase used. But the children had no interest in our songs. They just wanted us. They wanted to hug and jump and swing and talk and sometimes bite. Nutrition was not the only deprivation here. They had been starved of attention their entire lives.

Our work began to take a regular pattern. We came in the morning, we played with the children, we left in the evening. Sometimes we went to the bar and listened to the local men tell stories about Mama Ana. Most nights, however, we proceeded straight to bed, shattered and bruised from our hard days at the playground. And then we returned the following day for the same. It was relentless but it was gratifying. Cristina was always there, administering tissues and plasters and calming words. Mama Ana came and went with less regularity. She did not speak to us.

The more I saw Mama Ana, the less I felt able to define her. She was neither old nor young, neither big nor small. There were no unusual characteristics, nothing to mark her out in a crowd. She was simply Mama Ana, and that was all you needed to know. Her presence was her definition.

When she entered the sickbay on the second day of my illness, that presence was immediate and inescapable and left me nervous. She laid something down on the floor beside my bed.

'You have not been drinking enough water,' she said, examining the plastic bottle propped up on the sheets beside me.

'How do you know?'

'Who do you think brings it for you?'

I had not considered that any had been brought. Was this not the same bottle of water I had arrived in the sickbay with? I picked it up. It was fresh and unopened. I tried to twist the lid but my hand was too weak to grip. Mama Ana plucked it from me and opened it with one turn.

'You have lost a lot of fluids. Drink this now. I have left some bread down here, next to the bed. Eat it when you can. But drink this now. I will bring more.'

I took a large gulp of water. It tasted sensational. 'Thank you,' I said.

'For what?'

'For this.'

Mama Ana shrugged. 'It is what I do.'

I drank the rest of the water, ate the bread and then fell asleep.

When I awoke, Mama Ana was back in the room, cleaning the toilet. I felt hot shame.

'Please,' I said, 'you don't have to do that.'

'You can't do it,' she replied.

She was right. I barely had the energy to get out of bed. So instead I sought for a topic of conversation, something to distract from the glowering facts of her activity. 'Where did you learn English? You're very good.'

'Thank you. I learned at school.'

'Do all Romanian schools teach English to such a high standard?'

'I don't know. I am Bosnian.'

Something clicked inside me. Those men at the bar. They had called Mama Ana 'bozzy'. Not, as I had believed at the time, 'bossy'.

'Did you come to Romania because of the war?' I asked.

Mama Ana stood up from the toilet, turned around to face me, and smiled. It was the first time I had seen her smile, and it was neither pleasant nor unpleasant. It was just a smile. 'Yes, because of the war,' she said. 'Because the war ended.'

I did not know how to reply.

'I learned to be a nurse in the war,' she continued. 'I was good at it. At helping people. At caring. And so when the war ended and my country was free and at peace, I wanted to go somewhere else. Somewhere I could help and care. I read newspapers and called organisations and wrote to charities and I learned about the orphanages in Romania. In Bosnia they do not need my help any more. But here they do. Here I can care for these children for as long as they need me to. It is what I do.'

It was the longest thing Mama Ana had ever said to me. Indeed, it was the longest thing she ever said to me. By the following day, I had recovered enough to move back to the campsite and, another day later, I was able to return to work. I no longer needed Mama Ana's help, nor her care.

The children played delicately around me that first day back. They knew I had been sick. Instead of demands for chases and jumps and lifts, they hugged me or drew pictures on to torn pieces of paper and handed them to me as gifts, staring at me as I took them, beaming when I communicated my gratitude.

Cristina came and sat with us. 'Are you feeling better?'

'Much better. I have Mama Ana to thank.'

'We all do.'

'So you like her?'

Cristina looked shocked. 'Of course! Why would I not?'

'But I've heard such horrible stories about her.'

'Who from? The men in the village?' She snorted. 'They do not like her because she is foreign and she is a woman. And because she does not like them, and because she lets them know it.'

'So why are the children so scared of her? They fall silent whenever she's around.'

'Scared? They adore her! It is true they are less noisy and naughty when she is here. But that is respect. It is not fear.'

'They're terrified to even look at her!'

'Oh.' Cristina's shoulders fell back, and she studied me with what felt like pity. 'You do not understand. These children, they have been hurt very badly. All of them. So do you know what they do? They watch people. Very carefully. It is to see what you are going to do next – if you are going to hurt them. If they do not look at you, do not watch you, it does not mean they fear you. It is the opposite. It means they trust you. It means they do not have to look at you. And they trust Mama Ana. They know she will never hurt them. So they can ignore her. This is a rare thing. Even me, they watch.'

I exhaled deeply, expelling my misconceptions with my breath. 'I guess I got the wrong impression,' I said. 'Especially when you described her as formidable.'

'She is formidable! But only with adults. She will shout at those silly drunk men in the bar. She will be very cautious around new volunteers before she gets to know them. She has a talent for swearing at the authorities which is very impressive. But she never shouts at the children. She never hurts them. She only protects them. She only cares for them.'

'It's what she does,' I said.

'Yes! It is what she does. Come with me. I will show you.'

I followed Cristina through the playground and into the orphanage, cutting through the large dining hall, climbing a staircase and then walking down a long and straight corridor. Music came from the end of it, softly at first, echoing along the walls, growing in volume but not intensity as we neared.

'Look,' Cristina said, opening the door and gesturing for me to peer inside.

I did. Perhaps fifty of the children lay in clusters across the carpeted floor, eyes closed, fast asleep. Some twitched, others snored, but most lay silent and still. I had never seen any of the orphans so calm, so quiet, so at peace. In the middle of them all, Mama Ana sat cross-legged, her hands stroking the hair of the two boys nearest her, singing a gentle song.

'It is what she does,' Cristina whispered into my ear.

ABOUT CHARLIE

Charlie Carroll is the author of four non-fiction books: *The Friendship Highway*, *No Fixed Abode*, *On the Edge* and *Kapp to Cape* (with Reza Pakravan). He currently lives in Portugal.

————

Find out more about Charlie at:

W: www.charliecarroll.co.uk ♦ T: @CharlieCarroll1

07
THE KINDNESS OF STRANGERS

Finding kindness in the
strangest of places

Dan Martin

'I pondered on this desert hospitality and, compared it with our own... Their lavish hospitality had always made me uncomfortable, for I had known that as a result of it they would go hungry for days. Yet when I left them they had almost convinced me that I had done them a kindness by staying with them.'

Wilfred Thesiger, *Arabian Sands*

Kindness is no one thing. It comes in different guises and has different effects. It has no language and no bounds. It's everywhere. With increasing technology and self-reliance you can isolate yourself away from it, but it's in all of us to be kind and everyone is looking for opportunities to be kind.

Kindness is the fuel for travel. It's inescapable. It's a welcoming smile. It's being given directions. It's the offer of a room for the night. I have been lucky to be able to rely on such overwhelming kindness on all of my expeditions that I've almost become blasé about it. I've seen staggering acts of kindness as I've worked with refugees in Calais, Paris and Greece. As

Thesiger describes, I've seen people give me food and lodging when they had next to none and be so gracious about it that it seemed like I'd done them a favour by dragging my smelly, dishevelled body into their homes.

As you stray further from the beaten path, kindness increases. Cities tend to stifle people's kindness, possibly under the belief that someone else will help. Yet it's still there. You can find it in free hosting sites such as couchsurfing.com and warmshowers.org. You can find it in volunteers helping the elderly, the homeless, the young. You can find it in a clothes collection for refugees, a soup kitchen, a sports club. People want to be kind – they just need the opportunity.

On Christmas Day in 2014, I cycled into the Empty Quarter in Saudi Arabia and was hassled from one side to the other by people wanting to give me lifts, ply me with tea and stock up my water supply. I was looking for solitude and challenge in the emptiness but came away chubbier and with more friends than when I started. I pedalled from Sana'a to Mocha in Yemen, and despite the strain of impending warfare I suffered only at the hands of some of the finest cuisine I've ever tasted. From Yemen I crossed the once-pirate-infested waters of the Red Sea, again needing more insulin for sugary tea than insurance for kidnapping. In Djibouti I extended my stay couch-surfing from two days to six weeks while waiting for a bike part and felt welcomed at the beginning and like family by the end. In Somalia I was warned about cycling across Banka Gegriyaad, the Plain of Death, but was only put out by not being allowed to pay for my Coca-Cola (I had two). As the scenery changed through Ethiopia, Kenya, South Sudan and into Congo, the kindness held true. When my bike ground to a halt in Kisangani and I switched to public transport I was still swamped in hospitality. While two of the four engines on the wooden boat taking me up the Congo broke, detached and fell off, I was being stuffed with fresh fish and beans. As the train ran out of fuel, then passed through a bush fire before eventually derailing, my strongest memory would be of the tastiest green oranges that the tradesmen at the local market would accept no money for.

I met Fearghal O'Nuallain when I hosted him as he cycled round the world. In September 2015, Fearghal and I visited the refugee camp in Calais. It was dire. It was a field a few metres above sea level that is a former rubbish dump. It is the chemical spill zone for two of the surrounding factories and is in wet and windy northern France. The refugees there had made incredible voyages just to be held up by bureaucracy and 21 miles of seawater. They were all from countries where I had cycled and received nothing but the warmest of welcomes and yet when they came to Europe, to my home, they were left to sleep in a muddy puddle by a motorway. It was this trip that spurred Fearghal and I on to set up the Kindness of Strangers talks. After the 2015 talk I drove a van-load of jackets, jumpers, trousers and shoes down to Calais. The plan was to stay for two days but I ended up staying for seven months. It was great to feel like I was actively helping, like I was repaying some of the incredible kindness I had received. I'll never be able to repay it all but I intend to give it a go. The refugee crisis is the Great War of our generation. Now is the time to act; now is the time to stand up and be kind.

It's now February 2017 and we're still in the midst of the refugee crisis. I wake up most mornings in the Epirus region of Greece and the mercury is below zero. The country is under strain from the 60,000 refugees currently being helped here and yet I'm hopeful. Every day I see a patchwork of people from across Europe, across cultures and across political ideologies banding together to help out. Aid comes from all across Europe and the world; from grandmas knitting scarves to large corporations donating their end-of-season stock. The situation is stretched but it would be broken if it weren't for the kindness of volunteers, the kindness of strangers, plugging the gaps the strained system has thrown up.

ABOUT DAN

Dan Martin has cycled over 50,000 miles across three trips spanning some of the world's least visited countries, including North Korea, Somalia, Afghanistan, Iraq, Yemen, Saudi Arabia, South Sudan and the Democratic Republic of Congo. He spent two years working with refugees in Calais and Greece, and is now a master's student studying International Studies and Diplomacy at the School of Oriental and African Studies in London.

Find out more about Dan at:

T: @DanielMartinAdv ♦ I: @danielmartinadv

08
BE LIKE WATER

Women making waves

Easkey Britton

'We rode on waves of freedom, seeking our sense of self and place in the world, and we found it – in the water.'

Easkey Britton

'Water is life; it cleanses,' Farnaz said as we moved around the circle of women sharing experiences of what water means to us in our lives. We were a group of ten from very different backgrounds, ranging in age from 13 to 43. 'Being in the water makes me feel calm,' said Laleh. 'Water takes away my tiredness,' Mina added. This was the first time we'd met each other and for some it was their very first time to get into the water. They were hesitant and nervous but encouraged by the other women in the group.

These women were participating in the Be Like Water programme – an active, physical practice aimed at tapping into the more playful, creative and therapeutic qualities of water and the sea. Be Like Water was initially developed by me and Shirin Gerami (Iran's first female triathlete) with minority groups of women and girls in the remote Sistan Baluchistan region of Iran as a way to make surfing more accessible and to facilitate a greater body–self–nature connection.

One young woman's eyes were wide with fear as she stood by the edge of the water. She was in her early twenties and this was her very first time to be immersed in water. Shirin gently guided her into the water until it reached her shoulders and gradually encouraged her to take a breath and put her face into the water. At first, the young woman's fear of the water covering her ears was too great, until Shirin explained how everything sounds different underwater; that water makes its own music beneath the surface. Together, hand in hand, they took a deep breath and plunged beneath the surface. When they resurfaced, she was beaming and wide-eyed. 'I've never heard anything so beautiful,' she said, smiling.

How I came to be standing at the edge of the sea with these women in a remote part of south-eastern Iran is a story about connection – the connection and kind of bond formed between women with a shared passion and sense of adventure, women who create stories together of what's possible in places where it's supposed to be impossible.

It began when I met French film-maker Marion Poizeau for the first time in a hotel in Tehran in 2010. My decision to go to Iran in the first place was largely born out of curiosity – wanting to better understand the world through direct experience rather than being told how it's supposed to be. Often what we hear doesn't measure up to the reality of the actual experience. I was going on a surfing trip organised by a mutual contact. But the rest of the group dropped out or didn't make it for various reasons, including our trip organiser, who missed his flight. Marion and I were two strangers, on our own, stranded in Tehran. I had my surfboard and my customised surfing hijab; Marion had her camera. We immediately bonded, not willing to give up. We thought, *We're here now – what have we got to lose?*

This grittiness, or willingness to embrace the unknown, would go on to forge a close friendship and help us through many challenges and adventures in the years ahead.

We were heading for Chabahar, a seaport about a two-hour flight from Tehran in a far-flung corner of the country, on the Indian Ocean. We went not knowing what to expect, nor what the reaction might be to a Western woman surfing. We were going to a marginalised region of Iran called Sistan Baluchistan, with a distinct ethnic identity and a traditional, largely very conservative culture. There was no one surfing when we went that first year, and little did I realise what the consequences would be of becoming the first woman to surf in Iran.

When Marion put a clip online of the short film she made of that experience, it caught the attention of women and girls in Iran who were already engaged in various outdoor adventure sports, excited by the possibility of surfing. Surfing is synonymous with self-expression, creativity, the feeling of freedom that comes when we allow ourselves to surrender and tap into a natural force much more powerful than us – that's what we wanted to explore. We wanted to understand what it was like as a woman to pursue your passion and to experience surfing in your country for the first time.

Soon we became four – snowboarder Mona and swimmer Shahla joined us in 2013 to try surfing for the first time. Mona is a trailblazer in her own right, pioneering women's snowboarding in the country, and her petite size hides her explosive energy and enthusiasm in the face of any challenge. Shahla's elegance on land belies her fierceness in the surf – she's a natural waterwoman. That year they made history, pioneering the sport of surfing in their country. Yes, surfing in Iran was started by women. Considering the history of women in surfing, and the issues so many women face in the Middle East, the emergence of surfing in Iran through women is very important, and surfing is now seen by some proponents as something boys can do too (we were asked about this by a local boy watching us surf – the first time he had seen surfers, and they were women). The film that Marion and I made capturing that historic moment documents the story – a story that captures the beginning of an unexpected and ever-evolving journey since; the story of the first female surfers of Iran; the cross-cultural impact of surfing, the mixing of not just genders but social classes, religions and ethnicities; the generosity of the local fishing community at Ramin on the Sistan Baluchistan coast welcoming us into their homes, and their openness to try a sport like surfing for the first time; the shared experience of play in the surf that led to a kind of connection that transcended language and culture. A story that belongs to many and that continues to grow, with surfing now officially recognised as a national sport in Iran. It's a journey that can teach the importance of celebrating the beauty in our differences.

The ripple effect continued. The more we shared our story, the more we discovered the story of other pioneering women in sport. One of these women I 'bumped into' on Twitter. Shirin Gerami is no stranger to breaking boundaries. The same year we were defying the odds and writing the story of the first female surfers of Iran, Gerami became her country's first female triathlete when she competed in the 2013 ITU World Series in London. Her entry was by no means straightforward. She was granted permission to compete only in the eleventh hour, after a lengthy discourse with Iran's governing body, which lasted more than half a year. When she finally was given the green light, Hassan Rouhani, Iran's seventh president, was among the first to congratulate her when he tweeted: 'Shirin Gerami, 1st female triathlete to have participated in world championship wearing Iran's colours #GenderEquality.'

As someone who didn't surf but who loves the sea, Shirin offered a fresh perspective on the experience of the female body in water, stripping it back to the essence of why we do what we do: to connect more deeply to who we are; to shed those limiting beliefs and aspects of ourselves that no longer serve us; to lean into our fears instead of resist; and through this process of change connect more deeply with those around us and become more alive to our environment. The unpredictable, fluid environment of swimming, surfing and other water sports can take us out of our heads and into the sensory world of our bodies, allowing us to find our own sense of aliveness. As Yasmin, one of the girls who first went in the sea with Be Like Water, says, 'I feel like I am flying – out there on the water you don't think about any of your problems.' Through our shared watery experience, the idea for Be Like Water was born, which aimed to overcome barriers for women and girls who want to be in the water or surf – regardless of social class, religion, age, background or culture.

ABOUT EASKEY

Easkey Britton, an internationally renowned professional big-wave surfer, artist, scientist and explorer from Ireland with a PhD in Environment and Society, is channelling her passion for surfing into social impact and personal transformation. Her parents taught her to surf when she was four years old and her life has revolved around the ocean ever since. She is the founder of Like Water, a social-change initiative that explores innovative ways to reconnect with who we are, our environment and each other, through water. Easkey's work is deeply influenced by the ocean and the lessons learned pioneering women's big-wave surfing at spots like Mullaghmore in County Sligo. Currently a research fellow at NUI Galway, Britton co-leads the NEAR-Health work package on nature-based solutions, a framework to use blue and green space to restore health and well-being.

———

Find out more about Easkey at:

W: easkeybritton.com and likewater.blue
T: @Easkeysurf ♦ I: @easkeysurf and @likewater_blue

09
THE MOST SELFLESS MAN I'VE EVER MET

Loyalty, friends, commitment

Ed Stafford

In July 2008 I was depressed. I'd been walking for four months from the Pacific coast, up and over the Andes in search of the very furthest source of the mighty Amazon River, and then started down its length. I was weary, with tatty clothes and sore feet, and I was scared pretty much all of the time.

I'd entered the Red Zone – a lawless area where the Peruvian National Police Force dare not enter, which is ruled by drugs lords. The Red Zone is also home of several indigenous tribes who have been subjected to violent atrocities in the past at the hands of the terrorist group the Shining Path and consequently live in a state of hyper-vigilance against outsiders. Neither group was particularly friendly to me and both repeatedly told me that what I was doing – attempting to walk the length of the Amazon River – was impossible and that I would die trying to achieve it. Thanks, guys.

So I was depressed. I felt trapped by myself: I had committed to a mission, a potential world record, and I had told everyone in the pub back home that I was going to succeed. Some nights I would half dream, half mistranslate local Ashéninka people plotting to murder me under my hammock. Other nights I would simply cry myself to sleep with the only reassurance coming from the fact that I was infinitesimally closer to the mouth of the Amazon than I was the night before. I simply couldn't give up now – it wasn't an option – but I had no friends and I felt terribly alone. My childhood had also contributed abandonment and rejection issues of its own. The bottom line is that I was a walking shell of a man.

In a community called Pamaquiari, after being fiercely confronted by Ashéninka women (water thrown all over me, concrete shoved in my mouth, and red plant dye smeared all over my face), I met an anthropologist called Emily. Emily was Italian and had been granted permission by the Ashéninka people to live in their community to study their way of life. She was tall and beautiful and seemed like an angel sent straight from heaven to help me. Emily spoke fluent English and, after months of pretending to understand the people around me and becoming ever more paranoid and confused, suddenly I could speak and understand and joke and, dare I admit it, laugh.

Emily introduced me to a man who she thought might be able to help me. His name was Gadiel 'Cho' Sanchez Rivera and he was an out-of-work forestry worker who might want to walk with me. Cho and I sat down in his shabby kitchen and pored over my torn map of this part of Peru and estimated that I had about five days of walking to get out of the Red Zone. Cho agreed to help guide me out of the danger area.

Cho and I began walking together and immediately I knew it was a mistake. He was an evangelical Christian and began by singing religious songs at the top of his voice in Spanish. This was not only annoying – it was just plain weird – and I plotted to ditch Cho when we got to the next town.

But as we walked I could not help but realise that I wasn't scared any more. Cho wasn't scared – far from it – he both knew the area and 'was walking with God' and so he hadn't a care in the world. And it was seemingly contagious.

After five days of walking we walked out of the Red Zone and Cho said to me, 'I've enjoyed walking with you, Ed. If you like I will walk with you to the next town.' I thought about this – about the annoying habits he had, and about the confidence that he brought to our little team. 'OK, Cho,' I replied. 'Thank you.' And we walked together along the River Tambo for ten days to the next big jungle town – Atalaya.

In Atalaya I convinced my evangelical friend to have a beer with me to celebrate our last leg and we again approached the subject of walking. 'Ed, I've been thinking,' began Cho. 'If you want, I could walk with you to the mouth of the Amazon in Brazil.'

And so he did. Cho didn't go home for two whole years while he walked with me to the Atlantic Ocean.

Over the course of the two years we became almost like brothers. Cho observed my good moods and bad. He seemed to accept that I was under a greater pressure than him and forgave everything. In the evenings Cho fished and cooked, and I would collect firewood and light the fire. We enjoyed our roles and we worked well together as a team and so when Cho began to dream of learning English (we always conversed in Spanish) and visiting my country, I decided that I would try to make it happen for him.

We were drawing near to the end of our expedition and nearing the sea, and Cho and I would fantasise about the future whilst sitting around the campfire. On our more confident nights I would eventually become prime minister of Great Britain and he would become president of Peru. We let our minds run riot and came up with all sorts of initiatives that we would implement for our respective people and how we would be great leaders.

On 9 August 2010, Cho and I could smell the salt in the air. We'd been walking all the way through the night and knew that we were close to the sea. We rounded a corner and saw the Atlantic Ocean stretched out in front of us. Instinctively we shrugged off our packs and ran down the beach towards the waves. Also instinctively we started holding hands as we ran into the ocean – something that I wouldn't have dreamed I'd ever do, but perhaps sheds some light on how much of a cohesive unit we had become. For Cho it was an even more extraordinary day than for me because he had never seen the sea before. He had literally never tasted salt water.

About a month after the end of the expedition (with a little help from letters to the British ambassador in Lima from Sir Ranulph Fiennes and Michael Palin), Cho arrived at Heathrow airport with a scruffy bag of clothes and a big grin. He lived with my mum in Leicestershire for the next five months and played rugby for my local rugby team. At the End of Season Dinner he was even awarded 'Overseas Player of the Year'. He was, of course, the only overseas player in our team.

Cho will always be a brother to me. He took a pale, nail-biting, depressed tourist and decided to give up two years of his life to help him achieve his dream of walking the length of the Amazon. Cho always knew that by joining in month five he couldn't lay any claim to be the first man to walk the Amazon, but it wasn't about such egotistic goals for him. He wanted to live life, of course, but he knew that the best way for him to get the most out of life was to give. To give everything that he had: his courage, his knowledge, his time, his patience, his care, his whole life for two years. It's a display of selflessness that I've never seen equalled and I'll always be indebted to the ever-grinning man who sang those annoying religious songs.

ABOUT ED

Ed Stafford is the Guinness World Record-holding first man to walk the Amazon. Sir Ranulph Fiennes described his expedition as being 'truly extraordinary... in the top league of expeditions past and present.'

He was made European Adventurer of the Year 2011 and is a key face of adventure on the Discovery Channel with series including *Naked and Marooned*, *Marooned with Ed Stafford* and *Into the Unknown*. In 2016 viewing figures were 95 million viewers worldwide.

Ed has written two books, *Walking the Amazon* and *Naked and Marooned*, and in between adventures he gives motivational talks to corporates all over the world.

Ed was awarded the Mungo Park Medal by the Royal Scottish Geographical Society in recognition of outstanding contributions to geographical knowledge through exploration, and he is a global ambassador for Land Rover and the Scouts.

In 2015, Ed led Joe Simpson (author of *Touching the Void*) on a five-week jungle expedition into Burma, which was made into a BBC Two documentary broadcast in May 2016.

Ed is married to fellow adventurer Laura and they had their first child in June 2017, Ranulph James Stafford.

––––––––––

Find out more about Ed at:

W: edstafford.org ♦ T: @Ed_Stafford
I: @ed_stafford ♦ F: @edwardjamesstafford

10
THE WET FISH MEN OF THE BRITISH COAST

A story about wet fish, warm homes and learning to say yes to people

Elise Downing

It was late January when I met the wet fish man. I had been running around the coast of Britain for nearly three months and ticked off over 1,000 miles. It had been a wet and windy winter and now Storm Gertrude was in full swing. I was running along the North Devon coast following the South West Coast Path. The hills are brutal and the rain had turned the trails into mudslides. To make any upwards progress I had to claw my way up using bracken and barbed-wire fences. The hill itself would shield you from a headwind but as soon as you clambered to the top, you'd find yourself blown backwards. I had 22 miles to cover that day. The going was slow.

Seven miles in and I was ready to be done already. I was exhausted and bored and tired of fighting the wind. I knew that if I made it to Crackington Haven, around halfway, there was a bus I could catch to Bude, where my day was ending. I plied my legs on another few miles with the promise of catching that bus. I wasn't sure how that would fit into my overall plan. Going back the next day to retrace those ten miles would have put my whole schedule out of sync but the alternative was skipping a section and I wasn't sure I could deal with the lifetime of self-loathing that would entail. But I tried to forget about all that – *just get to Crackington Haven and you can stop running.*

I got there. I went into the tiny cafe for a can of Coke and a slice of cake. I thought about the bus some more but, now it was a real possibility, I couldn't bring myself to board it. I had already made that day's video diary atop one of those gnarly hills. Over the sound of the wind you could barely hear me but I was talking about the splinters in my hands from bracken and about having another 15 miles left to run. I didn't want to make a new video saying that, instead, I had given up. And so, before my legs had the chance to realise that our mind games were a lie and they had to move some more, I ate the last crumbs of my cake and set off up the next hill and towards Bude.

I don't remember much about the next section, just that it was cold and hard and included Scrade, one of the deepest and steepest valleys of the whole SWCP. After another seven or so miles of being chewed up, I was thrown out in Widemouth. It was easy from there into Bude, I knew from the map. A grassy cliff path, nothing too taxing. I couldn't do it, though. This time, I really was done. The light was fading and I didn't trust my tired legs out there on the cliffs, however sedate the path was. No bother, I could make up those last couple of miles in the morning.

But I still had to get to Bude, another three miles, where I was staying with local runners Annie and Graham, who had offered me their spare room for the night. I couldn't find a bus stop and my phone had done the annoying thing it always did and died as soon as it got even the tiniest bit cold. Then, suddenly, there – a glimmering beacon of hope, or at least that's how I see it now in retrospect – was the wet fish shop. I went inside.

'Are there any buses going to Bude?' I asked the wet fish man, so called for his position behind the wet fish counter in the wet fish shop.

'Yes,' he said. 'But you've just missed one and the next isn't for two hours.'

'Is there a path along the main road to walk along?' I wondered next.

'Not the whole way,' he said.

I had had enough hairy experiences on tight, fast Devon roads already to know that I wouldn't be risking one in the dark. I didn't know what to do. That about-to-cry feeling was surfacing in my throat. I needed to get to Bude but I had no idea how to get there and I was frozen and it was dark and everything was very lonely. Then –

'If you wait ten minutes,' he said, 'I can drive you down.'

Before starting the coast, I would have said no. However much harder it made things, I would have struggled on by myself rather than taking somebody else's help, feeling wary as to why they were offering it and worrying about being a burden. But I was slowly, slowly realising that better things happen when you let other people in. So instead I said, 'Yes, please, that would be great' and I stood by the wet fish in the wet fish shop and waited for the wet fish man to finish his shift, and then I got into his car to drive ten minutes down the road.

He asked what I was doing – and it was a fair question, I suppose. January wasn't exactly prime time for tourists and I had turned up in the wet fish shop just as it was getting dark, covered in mud and sweat, with my not-small pack strapped to my back. I told him what I usually told people: that I had run from wherever I had started out that morning, leaving out the hundreds or thousands of miles before that. Sometimes I just wanted to chat – not about the coast or running or adventure, just about normal things. Sometimes small talk is enough.

It was a Friday night and the wet fish man was heading off to meet some friends, I think, or maybe just heading home. I had expected him to just drop me in the centre of Bude but instead he took me right to Annie and Graham's front door. Bude isn't a big place but it's big enough that this was out of his way. I said thank you and goodbye and that was it. The wet fish man was gone.

I had never met Annie and Graham before. When Graham opened the door, he told me that Annie had been worried about me and headed out along the cliff to make sure I was OK. They hadn't needed to worry about me – I was a total stranger – but they had. Having been knee-deep in mud all day on the sodden coast path, I was directed around to the back garden to hose off before going inside.

'We have a hot tub,' Annie told me, 'if you fancy it.' Cold to the bone, there was nothing in the world that sounded better. And so, less than an hour after my panic in the wet fish shop, I found my tired muscles submerged in hot water, with a gin and tonic in my hand. Later we ate spaghetti together and talked about running and Cornwall and other trips, and everything felt a lot less lonely.

For a long time before setting off on my own big adventure, I followed along online as other people did big, exciting things. They were mostly overseas, exploring far-flung, exotic places. I watched them post stories about the hospitality they received in these remote destinations, saw them being welcomed into people's homes and fed and given a place to sleep and treated like part of the family. It was lovely to watch – heart-warming and refreshing and a welcome antidote to all the bad news and scaremongering we usually read about.

I wouldn't have that experience myself though, I'd been certain. This was Britain. People wouldn't open their homes and their lives up to me here in the way they might do elsewhere. It isn't in our culture. Instead, before I set off, I was questioned endlessly about how I would stay safe against all the bad people lurking around out there on those lonely coast paths. I had a safety tracker and was under strict instructions to check in with my dad every evening and tell him that I was alive. I was to be careful of strangers, remain purposefully vague about my location online. Be wary, expect the worst – that's the message I set off around the coast with in my mind.

Except, what I found – of course – was that Britain is full of wet fish men. People willing to go out of their way to make your day a little bit easier, who will sacrifice their own convenience to help you out. People who don't want anything in return but who, without even realising, leave the world a little bit friendlier than they found it. Occasionally you actually find yourself in a wet fish shop in your hour of need; more often it'll be an Annie or a Graham or an anybody else who rescues you.

What's for sure though is that you don't have to travel thousands of miles to find a wet fish man. There are plenty right here on home turf.

ABOUT ELISE

In 2015, aged 23, Elise set off to run a lap of the British coast. It was a journey of 5,000 miles and she was running self-supported, carrying her kit on her back. No woman had ever attempted this and Elise was entirely unqualified to be the first. But she found out that your legs can take you quite a long way if you let them and over the next ten months she explored both her home country and her own potential, developing a terrible fear of cows and a love of cake along the way.

————

Find out more about Elise at:

W: www.elisedowning.com ✦ T: @elisecdowning
I: @elisecdowning

11
CROSSING NOMADS' LAND

A 1,600-kilometre trek through
the Mongolian Gobi Desert

Faraz Shibli

I gazed down in horror at the big, brown monster between my legs: hairy, spitting and angry. My hips jolted forward, and I dropped down to the ground, as my first ride on a Bactrian camel came to an end.

But it took five minutes and four attempts for me to get off this creature's back, because every time it dropped down to the ground and I raised my leg to get off it, it jumped right back up, my crotch bearing the brunt of its force. No, my first encounter with the Bactrian camel was not a pleasant one. But it was the beginning of an adventure – one in which a group of other travellers and I attempted to cross the Mongolian Gobi Desert on foot with 12 of these animals for company.

Our aim was to walk 1,600 kilometres from the south-west to the south-east of Mongolia from May to July 2011 – a journey that would bring us most of the way across the world's most sparsely populated independent country and all the way across Asia's largest desert.

The team was made up of 12 people from ten different countries who had all met online – including a schoolboy, an ex-soldier and a female bodybuilder – making it as much a social experiment as a desert expedition. We had a crew of four locals to support us, including a translator and a cook, who would meet us along the route in a rickety Russian van.

And then, of course, there were our Bactrian camels – and even they were found online. Our leader viewed them via webcam, inspecting their humps, their feet and their teeth, and arranged to have them fattened up for months before we arrived. During the trek itself, they would carry our food, our water and some of our equipment. In return for this, they would routinely spit at, vomit on and kick us – as well as accumulate bloodsucking ticks the size of golf balls on their genitals that we had to remove by hand.

But they weren't all bad. These two-humped camels are simply built for desert travel. How? They can walk for up to ten days without water and carry up to 250 kilograms.

An ability to walk without water is a godsend in the Gobi. Spanning southern Mongolia and northern China, it is a rain shadow desert, meaning the Himalayas to the south block rain-carrying clouds from reaching it. It is a place of extremes, where temperatures soar to highs of 45°C in summer and plummet to lows of –40°C in winter. Its inhabitants are hardy nomads, who move their herds of horses, sheep, goats, yaks and camels with the changing of the seasons.

Both the dryness and enormousness of the land were clear from when we first arrived. For miles in every direction stretched a yellow, grass carpet: thirsty, threadbare and flat. In the far distance to the north and the south stood row upon row of dark, jagged mountains, like the plates of huge, sleeping dinosaurs' backs. But on the vast, arid plain, littered with tiny clumps of vegetation, we could look up and around without obstruction to an awesome ocean of deep blue sky. Never before on land had I seen so much uninterrupted space.

Herds of semi-wild horses galloped past us, steppe eagles soared above our heads and wolves howled in the hills as we slept. Despite its extreme remoteness, this place was full of life. Even people, though few and far between, appeared as if from nowhere: dainty women on tiny horses, wind-burned boys on rusty motorbikes and families moving to pastures new.

Mongolian nomads live in *gers* – small, wooden, collapsible yurts, which can be put up and taken down fast. With a mixture of curiosity and amusement about what we were doing in the desert, our new neighbours invited us into their homes, instantly making us feel welcome and providing a good reason for a brief but well-earned rest.

We listened to them talk about their experiences as herders – living lives of few possessions, closely interwoven with those of their livestock, on which they rely heavily for food, wool and transport.

In recent years, they had repeatedly faced a natural disaster called *dzud* – a summer drought followed by a harsh winter, which leads to many livestock starving or freezing to death. Less than two years before our trek, it had caused the death of 8.5 million animals and devastated people's lives.

Dropping deeper into the Gobi, we caught a glimpse of the fragility of their existence. Grass turned to gravel, gravel turned to sand and the mountains slowly disappeared. Skeletons of camels and horses littered the ground beneath our feet. For water, we zigzagged from well to well, many of which were dry. Forgoing showers for two months to save water, and with the mercury rising to 45°C at times, angry rashes emerged on body parts where they had no business. My ingenious, weight-saving plan to rotate furiously between just two pairs of socks and underwear had hideously backfired.

Even loading our camels became more of a chore, and some simply refused to carry. One even stampeded through our campsite, dropping precious food and water. At this point, I had sustained myself on a daily diet of little more than mutton, so constipation levels were critical – but nature's laxative came in the form of an 800-kilogram beast charging at me head-on and narrowly missing.

Sadly, the trek came to an end for some of my teammates who were kicked by our camels. The toll of walking just under a marathon per day also began to show and, as members of the team were evacuated one by one, our numbers slowly dwindled.

As those of us who remained reached the home straight, the worst of the weather hit us, including sandstorms and violent twisters that beat our tents, battered our clothes and covered everything we ate in sand.

But our spirits were once again lifted by the people we met on the road. Open doors, milky tea and wrinkled eyes framed by honest smiles punctuated their legendary hospitality – an absolute necessity in a country where roads are few, long-distance travel is tough and the traditional, nomadic way of life constantly demands it. It is even said that nomads can enter one another's empty *gers* on a journey and help themselves to food, drink and shelter.

People blessed us on our travels with toasts of vodka and produced gifts of dry curds, yogurt and fermented mare's milk to help sustain us to the finish.

Finally, after two months of trekking, four of us made it to a cairn near Sainshand in the south-east of Mongolia, having crossed the entire desert.

Although drained and thoroughly dishevelled, our load had been lightened by the men, women and children who called the Gobi their home. And, despite being removed from creature comforts and far from our loved ones, their many heartening acts of kindness made even the desert feel a little more like home for us too.

ABOUT FARAZ

Faraz is a British human rights lawyer and travel writer. He is a contributing author of *Mongolia: The Bradt Travel Guide* (3rd ed.), and in 2011, aged 25, he became the youngest Briton to cross the Gobi Desert on foot. In legal practice, he has represented refugees in the UK, including unaccompanied children and survivors of rape, torture and human trafficking, and he has acted as a consultant to the UN in Mongolia.

Find out more about Faraz at:

W: www.farazshibli.com/travel ✦ T: @shiblitravel

I: shiblitravel ✦ F: shiblitravel

12
FREE
COUNTRY

The start of a penniless
adventure the length of Britain

George Mahood

We were standing in our pants on the end of Britain. The sea chewed at the land around us, and the wind and rain attacked from all angles. We had the skin of freshly plucked turkeys. Starting a journey to cycle 1,000 miles to the top of Scotland without any money, clothes, shoes, food or bikes suddenly felt like a really stupid idea.

Land's End is frequented by three types of people: disillusioned holidaymakers who imagine that a trip to Britain's most south-westerly point is a rewarding experience, tourists who arrive there by mistake when they run out of road and those who are starting or finishing the popular Land's End to John o'Groats expedition. We fell awkwardly into the latter category.

The plan was simple. We had three weeks to get from the bottom of England to the top of Scotland – by foot or by bike – without spending a single penny. Setting off in just a pair of Union Jack boxer shorts, we hoped to rely on the generosity of the British public to help us with everything from accommodation to food, clothes to shoes, and bikes to beer.

My travelling companion was Ben. I asked Ben to join me on my Land's End to John o'Groats trip because he was the only one of my friends that fitted the necessary criteria; he was a self-employed layabout like me who did not need permission to take three weeks off work at short notice.

We started early, at about 7.30 a.m., in order to minimise the amount of people that would have to witness our scrawny bodies. The coastline around Land's End is impressive, but there is no sense whatsoever of being at the end of the country. Try standing there in your pants in the wind and rain in September, however, and it definitely heightens the experience.

The footpaths around the Land's End site were not designed with the barefoot walker in mind, and the heavy gravel cut into our feet at every step. In fairness, it is unlikely that many visitors to that part of Cornwall come without shoes. Even the notorious Naked Rambler wore a pair of walking boots. The cheating bastard. You can visit his boots – if you are really bored – in the End to End Story museum, which forms part of the Land's End complex. He is mentioned alongside Ian Botham, who has famously walked the route twice, and next to the story of a man who tried to push a pea with his nose the entire way. He got about two miles before he realised that it made his nose hurt.

We met up with Jemma, the End to End coordinator. Jemma had possibly the most enviable job in the world. Her working day involved sitting in a little office by a log fire, looking out to sea. She occasionally had to say 'Good luck' to people like us who were setting off to John o'Groats, or 'Well done' to those who had finished their journey. This, it seemed, was all she did. I was incredibly jealous.

We asked her if she had any interesting stories of fellow End to Enders, and she told us about a cyclist being hit by a car and killed, and another one concerning a group being robbed at gunpoint. These were not the inspirational, feel-good stories we were hoping for.

The idea of the penniless challenge was founded on the belief that, as a nation, we have lost sight of the basic values of humanity and kinship. We tend to be very suspicious of those that we don't know, and of anything that falls outside the realms of normality. Britain is broken, or so we are led to believe, and every unfamiliar face masks an axe murderer or terrorist. We choose to close our doors and hide from the outside world.

I wanted to prove this notion wrong. I strongly believed that there was still a lot of good to be found in society, and that there lies within everyone the desire to help others. By travelling without money and provisions, we were putting ourselves completely at the mercy of people we had never met, relying on their generosity to get us through. The Land's End to John o'Groats challenge is an iconic British journey, and it seemed to tie in perfectly with the penniless format of the trip as it encapsulated the whole of Great Britain.

Clothes were a priority.

We stood little chance of getting food, accommodation or bikes with our pasty bodies on full show. Also, it was bloody freezing and we didn't want to become the first people to die at Land's End before crossing the official start line. Although, if we had, Jemma would have had another story to tell other End to Enders before they set off.

'Well, if you make it past the visitor centre,' she would say, 'you'll have done better than George and Ben. They died right here in their pants.' It would have made her day.

We wandered aimlessly around Land's End not knowing what to do or how to begin the ridiculous challenge that we had set ourselves. After a few minutes of roaming we got talking to the only other weirdos who had decided to visit Land's End at 7.30 a.m. on that unforgiving morning. They were Australian. We explained to them why we were standing there in our pants.

'Strewth, and we thought people back in Oz were mad,' said Bruce.

'Crikey,' said Sheila. 'Bruce, go and get that old T-shirt from the car for these fellas.'

'No worries, Sheila,' said Bruce.

Bruce and Sheila were not their real names. Their actual names were lost in the wind somewhere.

Bruce and Sheila were halfway through their five-week world tour and had been in England just two days. Why they had decided to come to Land's End we had no idea. They were in their early forties and were travelling with another couple, Kylie and Jason, and the four of them were dressed like a mountain rescue team, as southern-hemisphere visitors to England tend to dress. Only a few square inches of their faces were exposed to the elements, but this was enough to see their caring and genuine smiles.

Bruce returned a few minutes later with the T-shirt. It was a momentous occasion – our first freebie and we hadn't even asked for it. The T-shirt itself was an XXXL made of silky white polyester, with a cigarette burn in the back and an inescapable scent of Australian body odour. I tried it on first, as Ben seemed more comfortable than me prancing around Land's End almost naked. It was ridiculously big and made me look like I was wearing a parachute.

The T-shirt did make a huge difference, however. Not only did it repel some of the icy temperatures that were being thrown at us, but it also transformed my confidence. I was instantly changed from a shivering fool in a pair of Union Jack boxer shorts to someone that was about to cycle 1,000 miles to the top of Scotland. The fact that I was still only half clothed and didn't have a bike was purely incidental.

We thanked Bruce, Sheila, Kylie and Jason and urged them not to judge England by Land's End, or the English by us. We decided to make our way to the Land's End Hotel, as it was the only place likely to be open so early. We had high hopes of raiding the lost property for some more clothes.

On our way to the hotel, Bruce's friend Jason caught us up.

'G'day again, guys. I got this for ya too,' he panted and handed us another T-shirt. This one was cotton, clean, white, without cigarette burns and a cosy medium fit.

I regretted hastily grabbing the first one. Ben gave me a smug grin.

The Land's End Hotel is a fairly ugly building, and is therefore in keeping with the surroundings. The interior, however, is rather posh and the reception area was crammed full of elderly American tourists who had been lulled there by the notion that it was a charming hotel perched on the edge of the country. There was an air of deep disappointment in the room.

We shuffled nervously towards the reception desk. The Americans shuffled out of the door through which we had just come, ready for their day of fun.

The hotel receptionist forced a smile when she saw us. She was in her late thirties and had the look of a supply teacher who would take no shit.

'Hello... Ruth,' I said, spotting her badge and dropping her name into the conversation like a sleazy salesman, 'I wonder if you can help us.' Her smile disappeared and she began to look panicked. 'We're about to attempt to cycle to John o'Groats without spending a single penny...' Her face turned to mild bemusement as though she had just been told the punchline of a joke she didn't quite understand. '... And all of our food, accommodation, clothes and hopefully bikes will have to be acquired from the generosity of the British public,' I continued, sensing she was beginning to warm up, 'and we were wondering whether the hotel had any lost property that has not been reclaimed that we could possibly have?'

There was a long pause. A sense of relief passed over Ruth. My speech was over and she realised she wasn't being robbed, she wasn't going to have to sponsor us and we weren't asking her out on a date.

'OK,' she said, 'I'll see what I can do.' She disappeared into the back office and we were left alone.

A middle-aged man and his wife arrived at reception to check out. He was dressed in cycling attire and wheeling a bicycle. With some careful deliberation we guessed him to be a cyclist.

'Are you going to John o'Groats?' asked Ben.

'I sure am,' said the cyclist.

'I'm his support crew,' said his wife.

'We're cycling to John o'Groats too,' said Ben, standing shivering in a pair of damp boxers and an ill-fitting T-shirt.

'Really?' said the cyclist, who then gave a laugh as if to say '*you nearly had me there*'.

Although our goal was the same, the differences between us could not have been further apart. He had at least £2,000 worth of equipment, top-of-the-range Lycra cycling clothing, a lightweight Gortex jacket and a devoted support crew. We were unsupported, barely clothed and without any form of bike. Oh, how we longed for a couple of carbon-fibre racing bikes, waterproof jackets and a support crew. And the Lycra was strangely alluring too.

The cyclist's name was John and he was about to begin his second End to End trip. He had completed the trip with a friend a few years previously and wanted to do it again alone, with his wife following behind in the car. He was aiming to finish the trip in ten days. We imagined we would probably still be in Cornwall in ten days. Once he understood that we were serious about our trip, he took a keen interest in how we were going to go about it.

'You'll need some shoes and socks,' he said. 'Hold on, I'll be right back.' His wife took hold of his bike and he scurried out of the door. He returned a minute later with a pair of trainers and a pair of socks.

'Take these,' he said, worryingly out of breath for someone about to cycle to Scotland. 'I brought way too many pairs of shoes and I never wear these anyway.'

They were white leather trainers, slightly retro and a perfect fit for either of us. We thanked him gratefully and wished him luck for his bike ride. We had earned the respect of an End to End veteran and we had not even crossed the start line.

Ruth returned from the office holding a big box of lost property. She dropped it down on the reception desk in front of us and our eyes scoured eagerly over the contents like a couple of clothes perverts.

The first item that caught our eye was a pair of thick, woollen, pinstriped suit trousers. They were tailor-made to fit a big fat man. Ben decided I should have them, since I was the larger of the two of us. After trying them on, it was clear that there would have been room for both of us. Not only were they for a big fat man, but they were also previously owned by an extremely short fat man, or someone with a penchant for wearing their trousers at half mast. The trousers hung halfway down my arse, and stopped halfway up my shin. I looked like the love child of a gangster and a sailor. It was *exactly* the look I was going for.

Also in the box were two cardigans. Ben took the trendy, skimpy black number and I took the thick, granny blue one. We only took items that had been unclaimed for over three months, to make sure they weren't likely to be reclaimed. However, I'm pretty sure the 'finders keepers, losers weepers' defence would have held firm.

The final item of lost property that we acquired was a child's pink umbrella. We naively thought that it would be a shield from some of the rain for a while, and we thought it might also be a useful bartering item to swap at some stage of the trip. It proved to be neither.

We were delaying the inevitable.

At some point we were going to have to leave the relative comfort and security of Land's End and start our journey towards John o'Groats. We had scavenged as much as we could from the hotel and it was time to leave. On the way out we bumped into Jemma again. She was armed with two 'official' Land's End T-shirts, which she kindly presented to us. Normal people have to pay for these, but we had told her that payment for anything was prohibited in our world. We pulled these on over our cardigans and we were ready to go. Land's End – been there, done that, and now we had the T-shirts.

Almost fully clothed, we were about to begin our journey towards Scotland. The official start line is in the car park and not by the sign, as you would expect. Crossing it was certainly an anticlimax. Our farewell party consisted of two old ladies, but it turned out that they were just waiting for the toilets to be unlocked. Even so, they uttered a half-hearted 'good luck', raised their eyebrows and smirked at each other.

We were finally on our way.

I was dressed in my suit trousers, which I had to roll up around the waist to keep them from falling down to my ankles. I was also wearing two T-shirts, a blue cardigan, a Manchester United baseball cap (on backwards, because I'm hip), one trainer and one sock. Ben was wearing two T-shirts, a black cardigan, an England cap (on sideways, because he's rad) and no trousers. He was wearing the other sock and trainer. It was still raining, but the wind had died down once we had moved away from the exposed cliffs. It was cold but bearable.

The road climbed gradually away from the coast and the Land's End complex became a distant blemish on the landscape behind us. We had been warned that John o'Groats was just a rubbish version of Land's End, so we were in no hurry to get there.

Just as it was getting dark on the first day, we were given a rusty BMX with no brakes and a child's unwanted scooter. These were later upgraded to marginally more roadworthy bikes, and we arrived in John o'Groats, a little under three weeks later, having fallen deeply in love with Great Britain. We secretly always had been, but we were no longer afraid to admit it.

At every stage of our journey we were overwhelmed by the generosity of the people that we met, as they went out of their way to offer us food, accommodation, clothes, bikes, directions, beer or conversation. Britain is a melting pot of cultures, races and personalities, and this eclectic mix of characters should be embraced and celebrated. Britain is far from broken; it just needs a bit of love and affection.

And it's not just the people – Great Britain is stunningly beautiful too. We expected Cornwall to be pretty, and we knew the Scottish Highlands would be spectacular, but it was the bits in between that surprised us. There was not an inch of the 1,000 miles that didn't have an appeal. Even Runcorn had a certain charm. Nowadays, with cheap flights and the Channel Tunnel, it is so easy to disappear to some faraway land rather than explore all of the beauty right on your doorstep.

Our journey was never about money. Travelling without money was simply a way to put us at the mercy of those around us, and allow us the opportunity to meet people, see places, and have experiences that we would not otherwise have had.

It did, however, teach us about the endless opportunities that are open to us, even without money. It doesn't cost anything to get out and explore your local town. It doesn't cost anything to cycle or walk through the beautiful British countryside. It doesn't cost anything to stop and talk to people. It doesn't cost anything to swim in the sea or a lake, or to visit many of Britain's most impressive sights. It doesn't cost anything to ask for help. It doesn't cost anything to make new friends, and it doesn't cost anything to smile and have fun. It took this experience to help us realise that Great Britain is undoubtedly a Free Country.

ABOUT GEORGE

George Mahood is an award-winning writer. Specifically, he was placed third in his village fete's limerick competition (Under Elevens category) in 1988. There were four entries.

He is the author of *Free Country: A Penniless Adventure the Length of Britain*, as well as five other non-fiction books.

―――――

Find out more about George at:

W: www.georgemahood.com ♦ T: @georgemahood
I: @georgemahood ♦ F: @GeorgeMahood

13

BE BRAVE, MODERN PILGRIM; BE NEEDY

Ramble with me and my donkey through the past and future, over thorny thresholds, towards potent fury, and into the company of inspiring travellers, while we try to overcome the cowering discomfort of holding out our empty palms and our pilgrim shells

Hannah Engelkamp

I heard once that there are only two stories. They are called 'you go on a journey' or 'a stranger comes to town'. If you think about it that means there's only actually one story – the difference is just in who's doing the telling. For some millennia women's stories were of the 'stranger comes to town' variety, as they weren't allowed to do the travelling themselves, and had to hang around to be visited, quill poised at a fussy writing table, dust hovering in the undisturbed air waiting to fall, eyes trained on the gap between poplars at the far end of the grounds, ears straining for the sound of hooves on pea shingle. Or for other classes, hurried glances down to the corner from the front gate of the farm, the sooty colliery terrace, the well-swept, earth-floored croft.

It's a fine reminder to me that whatever I'm busy doing, I should get it over with faster and go dig out my backpack, make the most of my contemporary liberty.

I remember the story of stone soup – that was a good one. A stranger comes to town; it's an old story so it's bound to be a man, although maybe it's hard to tell either way under the rough old sackcloth shoulders and lank hair. It's a sweet, warm, midsummer evening, but there's an unwashed funk about the stranger, and along with the unnerving grin it's enough to have little old ladies hurry to shut their doors. One of them isn't fast enough, and the stranger gets a foot across the threshold, a few dirty fingers around the door frame.

'I'm sorry to trouble you,' comes the voice, maybe surprisingly articulate – not hoarse or drunk at all. 'I was wondering if you'd be interested in a bit of dinner? I was thinking of knocking up a pot of stone soup, and there'll easily be enough for two. You could have an evening off, catch up with your darning, or whatever. Make the most of the light. I just need to borrow a pot...'

She pauses, and the stranger knows he's in. '*Stone* soup?' she says.

'Don't tell me you've never had stone soup?' says the stranger. 'It's astonishingly delicious. Some people make nail soup, or axe soup, but I like stone soup best. Look.' And he opens up a hand to show a handsome, palm-sized, sea-smoothed stone, with a single quartz band around the middle. 'I promise I'll wash my hands first,' he says. 'It's been a long day on the road.'

The old woman shows him in, still a little reluctant, but curious, hungry, and already looking forward to a night off cooking. She fetches a pot and some water, and is sent to put her feet up while the magic happens. After ten minutes of clattering and whistling from the kitchen, she peeps around the door, unable to sit still; she's been a mother for 50 years.

'How's it going?' she says, and he looks up from the stove where he's stirring the stone around and around, rattling and clanking on the cast iron. 'Have you got everything you need? Did you get the gas on OK?'

The man ushers her back to her chair and then, as an afterthought, says, 'I noticed on the way in that your onions are about ready to dig up. And was that rosemary I saw growing by the gate? Plain stone soup is very tasty, but with an onion or two and a few of those herbs it could be even better.'

You can probably see where this is going. It carries on like this for an hour or so, on a gentle simmer, the lady drawn to the kitchen door every few minutes by the lovely smells wafting through the cottage.

'Who'd've thought stone soup could smell so good?' she says. 'I've got some smoked paprika at the back of that top cupboard there, if that'd be helpful? And help yourself to the vegetables in the basket.'

The man would usher her back to her chair, saying, 'I don't suppose you have a few lentils, do you? And would you mind if I put in a little of the leg of pork hanging in the larder?'

The summer night is beginning to get navy blue around the edges as the man calls her to the table, and fills her bowl with the finest soup she's ever seen. He sprinkles a handful of spiced croutons on top, and a few chopped herbs. She fetches the salt and pepper, and a jar of cream from her own cow, and the two sit and chat and eat until the sky is full of stars and the pot is empty. He stays the night since it's so late, probably on the sofa but maybe not, and in the morning retrieves the stone from the washing-up and heads back on to the road, waving as far as the corner.

I've heard the story called 'The Wily Pilgrim' too; not very pious behaviour from a traveller of God, tricking an old lady, rummaging in her drawers. When I walked around Wales with a donkey called Chico a few years ago, we found ourselves on pilgrim routes often. Three trips to Bardsey Island at the end of the Lleyn Peninsula, or just two to St David's in the south, were worth one to Rome – the strange geographical arithmetic of the virtuous. We went once around the whole perimeter, so that must make us one half and one third of the way to Rome, and perhaps redemption.

It's said there are 20,000 saints buried on Bardsey, which isn't even a mile square; fifth-century Celtic monks looking for quiet places to become hermits, and finding themselves on a highway of the faithful, scattered about with holy wells and churches, and highwaymen.

Pete and Sue invited us to stay in their 'pilgrim pod' cabin and gave me several scallop shells – the symbol of the pilgrim. The big ones, bigger than my palm, would have been used as a bowl or a scoop, held out in hope as pilgrims sought food and shelter from the locals. There would have been no guarantee of welcome, relief, a full belly. Pilgrims were known as palmers in the Middle Ages as they brought back palm leaves from the Holy Land, sometimes shaped into a cross. Palms are so named as they look like an outstretched hand, and both words journey to us from the same starting place but via different routes – the plant straight from Latin to Old English, and the hand via Old French.

In 1962 the Indian activist, pacifist and writer Satish Kumar walked 8,000 miles, from India to the capital of each nuclear state – Moscow, London, Paris and Washington DC – carrying a bag of tea for each leader and the appeal for them to sit and brew a cup before pressing any red buttons. Kumar believes that reverence for nature must be at the heart of every political and social debate. His teacher, Gandhi's spiritual successor, Vinoba Bhave, gave him a gift on departure: the instruction that he must take no money. I have long been fascinated by this most uncomfortable commandment. The gift of a thin skin, of risk and fear. Of complete reliance on thousands of as-yet unmet people.

And perhaps more importantly, Vinoba sent the gift to those thousands too, along an 8,000-mile line. The gift of a person in need, a dependant, the expectation of mercy; an outstretched hand and the rousing potential to fill it.

———

A friend of mine, Alex, has been walking for three years, winter and summer, around the coast of Britain and Ireland. He posted on Facebook that he hates that bit every morning when he has to say goodbye to more friendly people, who for the night before have shared their lives with him. He feels sorrow in bidding them farewell, and as he's been going for three years already, he's probably waved goodbye to well over 1,000 people.

I didn't feel that way. It was the lightest part of my day, finally having squashed everything back into my pack, disposed of rubbish, said 'thank you' until it was dry in my mouth, and at last, the open road ahead.

Maybe I'm not that good a guest. I still feel ambiguity towards all of the people who put me up. Indebted. Arriving on foot meant being empty-handed every time – no merry bottle of wine to chink cheerfully on the countertop on the way into another new home, a visitor clocking in. No bunch of flowers, or bring-and-share pudding.

I came to realise that I paid my passage in other ways – being a break from the usual, bringing stories and theories, merrily telling a calcified set of the best anecdotes with pauses as if I was choosing the wording for the first time – performing. And on a tired evening it did feel like work, although always a joyous sort. I like new company, and in any case I arrived so exhausted every time, feet hot and sore, donkey fractious and desperate to know where he could rest. Wet things just had to be dried, tools borrowed. If anything was offered, my animal self just reached out faster than my sluggish, weary manners and snatched the comfort.

Some food, some wine, boots off, clean hair maybe – the evenings were fun. But the morning after I was often shy. If only I was the sort of person able to slip off before dawn, leaving a posy of flowers on the doorstep – thanks for the jolly evening and I'll take no more of your time. But I generally leeched on until after lunch, sewing something, filming something, charging some batteries, breakfast offered and accepted, the whole pack scattered across a lawn or field or spare room.

I think I can pinpoint the moment that I became a chore to each person. Some poured their sweetness forth so lavishly the night before that in the thin light of morning they are empty and tired. Some have half an eye on the time, politely not mentioning what they ought to be doing if only we'd be going. Some have run out of topics; some sheepish about anything said with the looseness of a glass of wine. Shy about having been seen. Some earnest with more things to say, but already aware of a departure in the future. The awkwardness of an imminent lengthy British goodbye colours the conversation for hours before. Everyone uneven with not knowing how long it will take me to go. The weightiness of the last wafts and clinchers of conversation, the summary of contact, wincing at clichés.

And me, aware of all this, like social static. Trying to maintain the pleasant chat, acknowledge the subtext of the offered cup of tea, get everything back into bags, and not *take the piss* – that most British of terrors. Worse than anything else, the fear of inadvertently expecting too much, misreading circumstances, overstaying welcomes. *Really lovely to have met you! I'll send you those photos! Did you write down the name of that book? Lovely occasion!* And then the profound squeaking silence immediately after, backward-glancing in a Grandmother's Footsteps test of farewell etiquette. Into the silence, as loud as if it was shouted, I can hear them mutter, 'Phew! I thought she'd never go!' And turn, on to the next thing, jobs postponed, priorities recalibrated, ordinary daily concerns paramount, the encounter filed as a past experience.

Maybe I'm too sensitive. Maybe I'm getting worse with age, as life gets, despite my wishes, more transactional. Home gets more fortress-like, I get to know myself better, and meeting anyone else can't fail to be hard work. Travel is a challenge to myself, soft-bellied outside my hermit shell.

––––––––

Whenever we walked up on to land more than 600 metres above sea level, some magic happened. At this point we would have strayed into the new 'open access land', where there's a public right of access to mountain, moor, heath and down, or registered common land.

In this old land, with memories of common use, ownership eroded, bureaucracy downgraded, I often ascended out of ordinary time and into eternal time. As the last telegraph poles faded into the mist behind me and Chico, and signal ceased trying to reach my mobile phone, there was no litter, language or fashion to pin us to an era. There were only old stones, rolling very slowly over each other, obeying gravity. The occasional sheep loitered; it could have been its own grandchild or grandparent – who was there to mark their ovine generations? Who begat whom? The lichen grew; moss gathered. With the breathing of seasons, bilberries swelled, fell and shrivelled, went adventuring in the guts of rabbits.

The larks flirted over the bare landscape, egg to feather and bone to egg to bone.

The thrill of even this brief remoteness ran through me. If we'd stayed long enough perhaps we'd have found ourselves guests of the Iron Age people who lived there once, in the hilltop forts, piling the stones up again.

I leaned on a standing stone at the brow of the hill – whether ancient monument or recent gatepost, or both, I didn't know. I caught my breath and saw that before us was some sort of quarry, busy with people. Their purpose and diligence was evident, even from this distance above them, and they laboured with enthusiasm, some in protective clothing digging beyond low dry-stone walls, some bent over tables and engrossed in fine work. Two horses pulled a flatbed cart of rusty white goods, and Chico tensed slightly at the sight of them, but watched with interest. As I'd climbed there had been no sign that this hillside was anything but another rise on this beautiful stretch of coast. I hadn't known that beneath my feet was treasure.

Perhaps a young man in overalls would perch on a wall, and make conversation as we each rested; perhaps he is my great-grandchild. Maybe we've slipped forward, not backwards, and the Iron Age stones have been piled back up by many hands of the future. This man is relaxed, happy in his work and not flinching from a foreman's scowl. His people have made peace with themselves and each other at last, and the treasures they are digging up belong to everyone again, and no one. He gives Chico an absent-minded scratch while he asks about my journey.

'Walking, are you? On your year's Palming? It's good work, for sure, seeking out the solitary, reminding them of their own buried treasure. Forcing the locks on their front doors! Have you found many people resistant? I guess not so much these days, now the Palming's more established.

'I couldn't resist opting for the Unearthing. Despite all the controversy I thought it was too exciting to miss the chance. And it is a finite community service – we won't be sorting for ever.'

I'll ask him if he's found anything good today.

'So much! And we're able to borrow some of it, if we like. I'm signing out a plastic bag today – a clear one. I'm going to put it over some of my ailing seedlings at home, see if I can make them a little microclimate, warm them up.

'Mostly we're sorting though, and cataloguing. I've been stripping copper wire this morning – winding miles of perfect shining wire, heaping bright-coloured plastic sheaths in the next pile for melting; we're just so grateful to the ancestors for their gifts. To think of us from the middle of their dark age, to have the wisdom to know we'd value these treasures, and to keep them safe in the soil for us. Each excavation is like a message across the ages – clever objects they have made for us and saved.'

Realism is outdated, says Satish Kumar. 'Look at what realists have done for us. They have led us to war and climate change, poverty on an unimaginable scale, and wholesale ecological destruction. Half of humanity goes to bed hungry because of all the realistic leaders in the world.'

Walk. Travel. Keep a wide-open heart and expect good things. And behind your open palm and open face be fired along by potent fury at what's been stolen from you. It's not too late, and there is inspiration everywhere.

We Western holidaymakers laugh when we get home and share stories of being warmly and unexpectedly cared for. The shopkeeper who shuts the shop and walks you all the way to your accommodation, the taxi driver who takes you home so his family can feed you until you think you'll never eat again. Transactions that we understand, that become relationships that we don't. Your host's horror at the offer of payment – we find it amazing, slightly weird. We anticipate and resist the final bill, but can't quite cope when it doesn't come. We are left naked with our debt, might even try to force notes into pockets. Our Western bounty is disregarded; our material wealth is brittle, short-term, desiccating. Our coins are silly talismans of a temporary order, which we clutch in the face of this enduring, all-encompassing warmth.

We laugh when people are upset by not being able to give, but that makes lots of sense. For the receiver to refuse to be vulnerable, to claim not to need to be helped – it's a crass denial of what makes us all the same. It is rejection of shared humanity.

We are so badly out of practice.

But we knew it once, instinctively, easily, and we will again. Right now we walk through a hard world, of 'reality' that isn't. Look out for it, and be furious. Recognise it where you see it. The demonisation of need, false dichotomies, the 24-hour rolling news of people who cannot be trusted, freakish disasters, fraud, fear.

Notice the pressure to be self-centred and refuse it – it isn't who you are! Stockpiling, fearing the future, scrapping at checkouts. Question what you are being sold – exclusive luxury because you deserve it. Get angry about being divided – you deserve so much more. You deserve stone soup for every meal!

Satish Kumar had the benefit of having been instructed; pilgrims too were required by their higher power to set out.

Cultures where giving is unquestioned have the simplicity of it being just how life is. It is us who have the hardest time of all this, so take small steps. We must be the traveller with the stone, terrified of being thought wily. Be brave, modern pilgrim; be needy.

ABOUT
HANNAH

Hannah is a travel writer and editor. Her great love is slow, resourceful, human-powered home travel. One day she had an epiphany, bought a young and opinionated donkey called Chico, and walked the 1,000-mile circumference of Wales, despite realising too late that he couldn't – of course – get over stiles or kissing gates. She wrote a book and made a feature-length film about the experience, both called *Seaside Donkey*. She is currently struggling with being detained by motherhood, and finding endless similarities between donkey and toddler.

————

Find out more about Hannah at:

W: www.seasidedonkey.co.uk
T: @hannahengelkamp ♦ I: @seasidedonkey
F: @SeasideDonkey ♦ P: @hannahengelkamp

14
SEEDS OF
THE FUTURE

The foresight and foolhardiness
of forest conservation

James Borrell

The dull thud was quickly muffled by the dense red soil. Another and another followed, as Antonio worked the battered shovel deeper into the parched earth. Up and down the hillside, others followed suit. Slowly and monotonously carving out depressions in the slope until it resembled the pockmarked face of some celestial body, or a small ill-disciplined army digging miniature foxholes. Next to each was a small mound of soil laboriously chiselled from the ground like a pile of rust.

Leaning heavily on the roughly hewn wooden shaft, Antonio surveyed the scene, beads of moisture condensing on his brow against the unforgiving Malagasy sun. Facing east, endless rows of hills like this one clothed in dry yellow grass undulated into the horizon, reaching, at some indeterminate distance, the Indian Ocean. In stark contrast, less than 100 metres above us to the west, a foreboding forest edge stood sentinel on the ridge, peering down on the group as they laboured. Deep emerald leaves shimmered and swayed in the breeze, drinking greedily from the sunlight filtering down through flecks of white cloud. The dark forest seemed impenetrable and distracting, drawing wayward eyes deeper into the gloom. Within, it concealed myriads of species from agile lemurs to ponderous chameleons, almost all of which are found nowhere else but here, the island of Madagascar.

Stooping to the ground, Antonio reached down into the hole, and carefully deposited a small package of rich black soil. From the top sprouted a tiny cluster of fragile leaves, and around the base, wispy white tendrils as fine as hair searched haphazardly for purchase and moisture. Meticulously, he scooped the adjacent mound of earth back into the hole, taking care to place the richest topsoil guardedly around the roots. Heavy hands encircled the tiny stem, patting down gently, and a final scattering of leaf litter gave the young tree a short, but much appreciated, head start against the weeds.

This young sapling barely reached the laces of my boots. If, miraculously, it survived the first few vulnerable years, it could take a century or more to eventually reach maturity. Replanting a rainforest is a laboriously long process.

Nine thousand miles away, different people were planting different trees for different reasons, and just like in Madagascar, they had been at it for some time. Fine Scottish drizzle mingled with the mist to thoroughly soak this new batch of volunteers as they trudged their way across the moorland. Pallid grey crags rose at the valley head and the occasional call of a ring ouzel rang out like flints being struck together.

Bouncing on tired suspension, several hundred birch and pine saplings rode passenger for a hilltop rendezvous. Several years previous, they would have been collected in the vicinity as seeds. Carefully, these seeds were propagated first in polytunnels, and then out in the elements to acclimate them to the fickle mountain weather. The final stage was to rally volunteers to help plant them out. A few hundred here and a few hundred there has, over 25 years, amounted to over one million trees restored to the Highland landscape. A remarkable achievement for a modestly small reforestation charity aptly called Trees for Life.

Restoring forests – which in essence is simply planting the right trees in the right place, faster than they can be cut down or burned – is perhaps the most primal and practical of conservation activities, and there is still much to do. Global tree cover has declined by more than half, with places like Madagascar and Scotland each losing over 90 per cent of their original forests. Yet as obvious, necessary and prudent as it seems for society, forest restoration is a remarkable achievement for several reasons.

First, it requires within us a vision and environmental awareness of the deep past. As a species, we have a short societal memory. How many in the UK know that barely 30,000 years ago lions, mammoths and bears would have roamed the swamps where London now stands? Only 3,000 years ago, no human had ever set foot on Madagascar. The rate of environmental change, especially when it comes to forests, is matched only by the enormity of our ignorance. Incrementally, over lifetimes and generations, the erosion of our environment passes unnoticed. It is only when we compare that which we have now with the seemingly fantastical accounts of the past, that realisation dawns of how much we have lost. This is the malignant syndrome of shifting baselines, whereby we measure the state of the environment with our own recollections of the past, unknowingly concealing a profound decline. A degraded environment all too rapidly becomes the new normal.

Second, reforestation requires a level of ambition close to lunacy for the scope of the task to be realised. Billions of trees across millions of hectares and scores of countries. On the surface at least, this surely seems to be beyond the capability of any one person, organisation or campaign. Restoring forests is the moonshot for our generation.

Yet foremost, it requires time. Far more time than any of us is allotted in this lifetime. Reforestation is a fruit that no one here today will be alive to appreciate. That no one here today will be able to reap the benefits from or to marvel at its beauty. And so conservation, true conservation that relies on the long term, will only ever be a gift to strangers. Strangers in the next generations that we will never meet, who – if we do the job well – will find it impossible to distinguish that tiny seedling sown by hand from those precious fragments of original forest still standing. Thus our job is to be invisible. To take all of the satisfaction from working hard at work worth doing irrespective of what the future holds.

And so what is the motivation for the soggy volunteer in the Scottish Highlands or out on the sun-baked hills of Madagascar, or any corner of the world where conservationists quietly and tirelessly labour? Some say it is the desire to leave the world in a better place for their children's children. That conservation is the morally right thing to do. Others hark at the benefits: forests provide timber, food, shelter and sustainable livelihoods. They trap moisture, bring rain and prevent soil erosion. Where resources are more plentiful they can reduce conflict, and even in urban areas, greenery has been shown to increase health, happiness and improve our well-being. Me, I'm driven, to degrees, by all of these arguments, but as a conservation scientist I simply see the most beauty where mankind treads the softest. I remember the words of Delia Owens, who, fighting a losing battle to protect Zambia's declining elephant herds, wrote, 'Wilderness on earth is now so confined that you can venture only so far into its heart before every step starts taking you away again'. My aspiration is merely a long, uninterrupted walk in the woods somewhere, basking in the diversity of life on earth.

Shouldering the shovel, Antonio meandered wearily down the hill, tired legs veering left and right to avoid haphazardly placed seedlings. Back at camp a fire still smouldered ready to be rekindled. That night we shared a simple meal illuminated by flickering firelight as pale wafts of smoke lingered like ghosts in the canopy. We huddled together sharing stories of homes thousands of miles apart. One by one we retired to sleep that deep dreamless sleep that comes from outdoor exertion, with a trillion stars glimmering overhead. For Antonio, the number of trees planted or the project goals were both less important than the fact that people came a long, long way to help build a richer future between earth and sky.

When so many are searching for meaning and purpose in their deeds it's worth remembering that in giving kindness to strangers you reap at least as much as you sow in satisfaction. Sometimes kindness is as humble as planting trees; begin, repeat, and watch it grow.

ABOUT JAMES

James is a conservation biologist with a passion for adventurous fieldwork and expeditions. He's been involved with a range of projects over four continents, from critically endangered big cats in the remote Dhofar mountains in Oman to biodiversity surveys in the Peruvian Amazon and forest genetics in the high Arctic. James believes in the optimistic side of conservation. Instead of all the bad news we hear about daily, let's celebrate the stories that succeeded against all the odds.

Find out more about James at:

W: www.jamesborrell.com ♦ T: @James_Borrell
I: @james_borrell ♦ F: @Jamesborrell.co.uk

15
A TRIBUTE TO CRAZY LARRY

Never judge a book
by its cover

Jamie McDonald

Below is an extract from the book of my run across Canada dressed as the Flash, Adventureman: Anyone Can Be a Superhero.

———

Eventually we made it to the Stoney Nakoda Resort, which was in the middle of nowhere. A man with a huge bushy moustache and long, ragged hair appeared to give me a high five and shouted, 'My name is Crazy Larry!' He stamped his feet. 'Jamie, I've been searching for you for so long! You don't know how much this means to me. Jamie, you're my Christmas present!' He then stomped about in the busy hotel lobby with his video camera on, in front of lots of people, shouting: 'This is the Jamie McDonald – he's insane. I am with him – yes, I am with him. Do you know who this guy is?'

I remembered someone telling me I'd meet a guy called Crazy Larry out West, who doesn't have a fixed abode and cycles around constantly, and people treat him like some sort of pilgrim – they help him out from the goodness of their hearts. He's something of a local legend. He then asked me if he could cycle alongside me the following day.

I'm not going to lie, I was anxious about my run with him – he'd earned his nickname for a reason, after all. We were blown to bits by the 60-mph wind, but it didn't seem to dampen Larry's spirits. 'Man, I've never been in winds like this before – I feel alive!' He crackled with laughter. He reminded me of the way kids go potty in the wind. As we continued to scale the foothills, we almost came to a standstill, crawling slower than a snail.

Larry put his butt on the top frame of the bike so that his feet could touch the ground to keep him balanced. He must have nearly fallen off 50 times. He still managed to edge in front of me to try to cop the worst of the wind. It was a selfless gesture.

A wonderful surprise was in store for us: Robin Melling from the British Army Training Unit in Suffield. Of all of the army officers, Robin was the one who'd been the least happy about my run through the Rockies. But now, a month later, he was by my side, in his running gear, saying, 'I still think you are absolutely mad, but can I run with you?' It was good to have a voice of reason to counter the eccentric Larry. I could see Robin trying to measure up Larry to check he was all there, as most people do when they first meet him.

A few more miles went down, inch by inch, and I noticed that the mountains around us were getting higher. 'Jamie McDonald!' whooped Larry. 'You are officially in the Rocky Mountains – you've made it. Say hello, my friend, because the mountains are saying hello to you!' The three of us battled into a steep incline on the fringe of a valley. The wind was behaving like a turbine, channelling all of its condensed power into a narrow corridor. Robin and I took it in turns to run with Caesar (the name I had given to the chariot I used to push all my stuff along), although quite a few times Robin would refuse to let me take him back. 'Don't worry. Use my energy while I'm here.'

Larry started singing, rhythmically but also maniacally. I thought he was finally about to lose what few marbles he had left. 'Ain't nothin' gonna break my stride. Nobody's gonna slow me down, oh no, I got to keep on movin'. Ain't nothin' gonna break my stride!' He rustled up dormant emotions in Robin and me and, before we knew it, we were all singing our hearts out. 'No one's gonna slow me down, oh no!' Robin started to use his hands as though he were swimming through the wind; Larry had broken his scepticism down too. How ludicrous we must have looked: one guy dressed as the Flash, the second in luminous biking gear and the third clad all in black like an undercover agent, all singing and dancing down one of the busiest highways in Canada.

Robin's wife, Charlotte, and their two children, Harry and Ben, joined us to run the last half mile. At the Copperstone Resort at Deadman's Flats, Crazy Larry initiated some hip-hip-hoorays with everyone joining in.

After the usual five hours' sleep, I bumped into Larry in the lobby. His grin was as wide as his eyes. 'Are you ready?' he asked, like a wrestling referee. We hit the road to Canmore, a town encircled by gorgeous snow-topped peaks.

Larry would talk and talk and when he got bored of talking, he would talk some more. Occasionally, he'd play music on his phone and sing along to it. He put on 'Isn't She Lovely?' and nodded his head like Stevie Wonder does. It wasn't quite the tune to propel me forward, but nonetheless the singing passed the time. Often we would lose our breath and double over from laughter, which is not the thing to do when you're trying to run a marathon through the Rockies. I wondered whether Larry was in fact a sports psychologist who'd been planted on my route to help keep me going.

We went to the Communitea Cafe in Canmore for a spot of lunch. Larry gathered together all sorts of people to cheer and applaud us. I met Clara Hughes, a six-time Olympic medallist in cycling and speed skating. With all the buzz around us, we were unable to have a proper chat, but I later discovered that Clara sent out this delightful tweet:

'Just had a chance to say hi to a wonderful human being in Canmore. He's run all the way from Newfoundland! I think he makes people smile wherever he goes. Canada is lucky to have him travel our land!'

Being tweeted by an Olympic medallist was another great honour.

As I was devouring some delicious pad thai, some little girls came over to say hello. 'Did you know that no girl has ever run across Canada before?' I said. Their faces all lit up. 'Let's hope we see a girl run across Canada in the near future. I think it would be awesome for Canada and the world.'

Larry and I carried on towards Banff, joined by a very special runner. Colin Harris ran across Canada a few years ago in aid of Take Me Outside, a campaign to tell children to stop staring at screens and get outside. It's a brilliant message, I think. As we ran together, Colin told me all about his journey. He'd had a support vehicle for all but two months of the trip. He'd have to park up, run and then hitch-hike back to his vehicle.

'That's pure determination,' I said, with my arm around him. 'Did you have any emotionally difficult times?'

'The first day I ran with my dad driving alongside me. I covered thirty miles and he got out of the car to say that nobody would ever understand what I was going through. And then my dad began to cry. It was a seriously proud moment for both of us.'

I thought about my own dad, whom I'd be seeing very soon. Then Larry cycled in between us with his massive smile, shouting at the top of his voice, 'Can you feel the love? Can you feel it? I'm feeling the love!'

Near Banff I had to tell Larry that it was time for me to continue solo. I think he would have cycled with me all the way to Vancouver and then probably got on the flight home to England if I'd asked him to. It was a sad time because, for three consecutive days, Larry had been by my side and I'd come to love his huge moustache, big heart and chirpy personality. His charisma had helped me to conquer a major part of the Rocky Mountains. As tough as it was to say goodbye, this journey was about letting people go, and allowing new people in. But there's only one Crazy Larry and I'll never forget him.

ABOUT JAMIE

Jamie McDonald is a world-record-holding adventurer, author and motivational speaker and the founder of Superhero Foundation. He lives in Gloucester, and was voted one of *The Independent*'s top 100 happiest people in the UK.

As a child, Jamie spent the first nine years of his life in hospital with a rare spinal condition, syringomyelia. In 2012, Jamie began an adventurous fundraising quest to give back to the hospitals that helped him as a child by cycling 14,000 miles from Bangkok to Gloucester on a second-hand bike bought for just £50. Jamie cycled through more than 20 countries and was shot at when caught in the middle of a military firefight, arrested by wary border police and forced to sleep rough. Jamie then attempted the world record for cycling non-stop on a static bike. Jamie stepped off the bike as the Marathon Static Cycling Guinness World Record holder, having cycled for more than 12 days. He raised more than £20,000 during the two challenges.

In 2013, Jamie became the first person to run the 5,000 miles (equivalent to 200 marathons) across Canada without a support crew (and dressed as the superhero the Flash) – raising more than £250,000 for children's charities along the way.

—————

Find out more about Jamie at:

W: www.jamiemcdonald.org ♦ T: @MrJamieMcDonald
I: @mrjamiemcdonald ♦ F: @jamiemcdonald.org

16

THE DIFFERENT FACES OF KINDNESS

Acts of kindness are more common but less spectacular than you think, and that's a good thing

Julian Sayarer

My twenties saw me cycle about a half-dozen times across Europe, always journeying east to my second nation, Turkey, and the city of Istanbul. Before and since the first of those rides, I hitch-hiked and trekked my way through a number of other journeys that took me across Europe and parts of the United States. Whatever the number and extent of those journeys, however, the thing that most people – certainly in adventuring circles – continue to know me for is a 2009 circumnavigation in which I set a world record for cycling around the world; a ride that – endearingly and seemingly quite enduringly – earned me the epithet 'angry young man'.

That ride was 18,049 miles in 169 days, 20 countries, an average of 10 euros and 110 miles – my daily budget of currency and distance, respectively. And it was amazing. Whether writing or speaking about the trip, I tend to rattle off these figures at the outset; I mostly see them as distractions from the human richness of all that I encountered. Across those miles, the number of instances in which I was helped by people – strangers – is far, far too numerous to mention them all individually. I often wonder if I am doing them a sort of vulgar disservice when I itemise a list, as if crowning the absolute kindest moments, of what were each of them the most surprising and heart-stoppingly kind, generous and warm-spirited gestures.

I was helped by many who could afford it. I was helped by others who probably could not. Others, and this is probably the majority, did not really go out of their way to help me so much as they proved willing to trust that I would do them no injustice or harm, and so they would be no worse off for sharing with me what was theirs.

Of all the kindnesses, I find myself thinking of this third category the most. An Oklahoma truck driver found me and my permanently puncturing tyre at a New Mexico rest area on Interstate 10. With my bicycle strapped to the back of his cab, he drove me the few dozen miles to the next town where I could buy the replacement for my broken pump. In the steppe of Kazakhstan, without the shade of a tree or building for many hours' riding, a family invited me into their yurt for shelter from the oppressive sun and heat, and to share a bowl of chilled soup for lunch.

Strangers in Texas paid my restaurant bill unannounced; strangers gave me money at roadsides when they heard what I was doing and wished to buy me a meal. Stunning generosity humbled me all around the world (most commonly of all – it should probably be noted – in the Muslim world), but far and away the most valuable lesson, in a public debate now gripped by dread of strangers, was the fact that nobody, not one person, really did me wrong and just about everyone wanted to see me right. That is the world in which we live, and it is that plain and very pragmatic reality that now feels to me more tender than any one anecdote, no matter how staggering, that I now prefer to keep to myself. Those acts I now hold to more as the personal treasures and moral lessons by which I hope and try to live my own life.

When I cycled around the world, earning that moniker for my supposed anger, I did so under the banner of 'This is not for charity'. This title, as some took it, wasn't intended to be antagonistic – it was simply born of a faith that the good in the world is, and needs to be, the rule and not the exception. In the modern world, full of complexity and compromise, charity is seen as a safe place; a place of uncontested good into which we pour our dreams of something better. Cycling hundreds of miles through deserts and mountain ranges, and along ocean coasts, always in love with such an existence, now and then I would consider the concept of the charity bike ride. What came back to me most often was the contradiction in the notion that we can dress up our ultimately quite selfish desire to see the world, to do something wonderful, as an act of altruism. Sure, perhaps both can be true at the same time: we have some fun for ourselves, and raise some money for a decent cause. I see the logic there, but even with that, some depictions of charity bikes rides – all sentiment and hardship – still grate at my nerves. The idea that people should sponsor a cause because the rider is 'out there' suffering will always seem to me dishonest. Even if some are perhaps less likely than me to enjoy life by bicycle quite so much, still, it feels like there is too much genuine suffering in this world for Westerners to start talking of voluntary bike rides in those terms.

The record I broke had been set in conjunction with banks, investment funds and other big businesses – with a charity component on the side. I saw in that record attempt all the images of life on the road, images that I felt in part belonged to me, being used merely for corporate gain. The kind strangers helping you out, the peace that can be found in travel – all of it was being reduced to a piece of marketing for corporations that invest in bombs that destroy, in medicines sick people cannot afford, in mining companies that sink mines and wells on the lands of some of the world's poorest, altering climates as they do so and as they drill.

None of that had been mentioned in the record that I set about breaking, and I felt that – as citizens of countries mostly safe and relatively very prosperous – we adventurers, if that's what we're to be called, have to do better. We are all sufficiently aware of, and increasingly impacted by, the world's ills, in such ways that they grow ever harder to ignore. I've never accepted the idea of two worlds: one 'out there', where strangers are good and people are kind; and another of business as usual, where we tolerate so much suffering of others as part of a normality, a daily grind that even we do not ourselves enjoy so very much.

To learn those lessons of the open road, and to try to bring them back into our own societies, became for me the product of my travels, and that is still a bigger and more worthwhile challenge than scaling roads, rivers, mountains. Not quite sure who to thank from my own 18,049 miles of kindnesses, I dedicated my book of the journey, *Life Cycles*: 'For all the strangers.' We are all one another's strangers, people just waiting to be met, and unbreakably bound inside the same very special network of our species on this strange, blue-green orb. As individuals but also in the societies and politics we build, we must be kind to one another.

ABOUT JULIAN

In 2009 Julian broke a world record for cycling around the world, and is still working on not being defined by only this feat. The story of that world record is contained in his first book, *Life Cycles* (2014), while *Interstate* (2016) chronicles a hitch-hiked journey between New York and San Francisco and won the 2016 Stanford Dolman Prize for Travel Book of the Year. His other books are *Messengers* and, most recently, *All at Sea*, a Royal Geographic Society Book of the Month.

———

Find out more about Julian at:

W: juliansayarer.com

T: @JulianSayarer ✦ I: @juliansayarer

17
THE BANKSY OF BANGLADESH

A rare example of kindness and humanity amid a crisis known only for its savage acts of inhumanity

Katie Arnold

That August morning had started just like any other for ten-year-old Noor Kajol. She rose from the bare wooden floor where she slept, just as the sun cast its first rays across the emerald paddy fields behind her house. She ate breakfast with her mother and four siblings, crouched around their wood-burning stove and then ran outside to find her father.

He was the village woodcutter and a gentle man, whose attempts at authority always faltered in the presence of his only daughter. She had deep brown eyes and a vulnerable stare that could infiltrate the soul of any man, let alone her father. That morning they brushed their teeth side-by-side, flicking water at each other with wide, soapy grins, until a deafening crack forced her father to the floor, blood streaming from a bullet wound in his head.

Noor Kajol and her family belong to the Rohingya ethnic minority, a group of 1.1 million Muslims who have lived in Myanmar – a Buddhist-majority country – for centuries. They are neither wanted nor recognised by the Myanmar government, who stripped them of their citizenship rights in 1982.

The majority of Rohingya live in northern Rakhine State, a deeply impoverished corner of Myanmar where they face severe restrictions on their freedom of movement, limiting their access to livelihoods, healthcare, food and education. These restrictions have been strictly enforced by the state's security forces, who have arbitrarily arrested, extorted and tortured the Rohingya with impunity.

On the 25th August 2017, a Rohingya insurgency launched a series of attacks on government outposts in northern Rakhine State. The military's response was swift, brutal and indiscriminate with thousands of innocent Rohingya thought to have been killed and hundreds of their villages burnt to the ground – including Noor Kajol's.

With flames licking at her heels and the sound of bullets cutting through the air, she fled her family home, leaving her father's body to burn amid the bloody chaos. After three tearful days walking through the thick Myanmar jungle, Noor Kajol crossed into Bangladesh with her five remaining family members. In the six months following those August attacks, nearly 700,000 Rohingya Muslims were forced into Bangladesh.

On the night it kicked off, entrepreneur Mehedi Chowdhury was online searching for a new car. For three long years he had sat behind a computer screen in a darkened room, building his software company from scratch. With ten clients now on the books, it was time for a reward. Months of dedicated research lead him to the Nissan Sylphy and in a few weeks' time he hoped to be navigating the congested streets of Dhaka – the capital of Bangladesh – within the car's spacious interior.

One evening, while considering the four different colour options offered by Nissan, Mehedi looked across at the television to see streams of tired and hungry people crossing into Bangladesh. As the reporter spoke about the atrocities being committed in Myanmar, the Rohingya refugees could be seen scrambling for a space on a forested hillside where they would construct a primitive shelter amid violent monsoon rains.

Within a few days, Mehedi had spent all of his savings and was on a flight to Cox's Bazar – the epicentre of the refugee influx.

'There are only so many times that you can watch all these videos of people being beaten on Facebook without doing anything about it – I had to go there and help. I am a human being after all.'

Those first few weeks in Bangladesh were the toughest for Noor Kajol as the humanitarian agencies were overwhelmed by the influx and struggling to muster sufficient resources. Her family slept on the sodden floor beneath a single sheet of tarpaulin, which hung precariously from two trees. She had to walk for miles to find a private place to defecate – while others preferred a spot by her tent – and, crucially, there was no food.

Each day she would walk to the main road and beg for food with her four siblings. The entire 60-kilometre stretch from Rajapalong to Teknaf was lined with ghostly figures like Noor Kajol, their emaciated hands poised in their air as they waited for vehicles to pass. The sound of car horns and the choking smell of diesel alerted the refugees to their imminent arrival, and they would flock to the middle of the road and jostle for prime position.

On one occasion Noor Kajol was wrestled to the floor after catching some bread thrown from a passing tuk-tuk. An older boy emerged from the tussle proudly clutching the misshapen roll. She ran away in tears and with the crowds swelling, decided not to return.

Once Mehedi arrived in Cox's Bazar, he rented a small truck and joined the caravan of vehicles clogging the rural Teknaf road. For hours each day he would hand over his savings – now in the form of 500 tents and 500 food parcels – to the desperate faces below.

On his last night in Cox's Bazar, a thousand Rohingya refugees surrounded his truck. Each food parcel thrown to the crowd initiated a tense and sometimes violent struggle. As the delivery ran low, refugees clambered on board the truck, seizing whatever goods they could find.

Fearing for his life amid the frenzied stampede, Mehedi cowered at the back of the truck. As the final parcel disappeared into the crowd, a Rohingya refugee pulled Mehedi to his feet and thanked him for the food. Without the generosity of people like him, the elderly man said, they would not have survived the first few weeks of the crisis.

The next day Mehedi boarded a plane and returned to the familiar embrace of Dhaka. But his thriving business and beloved computer screens did not offer him solace for long. Over the next few months he would make three more trips to Cox's Bazar with donations from friends and family across the world.

'I always thought of myself as an introvert; that is why I started a business which let me sit behind a computer screen all day. But working with the Rohingya showed me the value you can get from meeting people from different walks of life.'

———

After a few desperate weeks, humanitarian aid flooded into Bangladesh. The multicoloured trucks hired by individuals like Mehedi were replaced by shiny 4x4s, branded with official acronyms written in white and blue. The refugees retreated from the roadside, waiting instead in orderly queues while men and women in branded T-shirts distributed large sacks of rice. Eventually, the Bangladeshi government prohibited its people from voluntarily distributing food.

Noor Kajol and her family were relocated to the Kutupalong refugee camp – a tent-city of over half a million people that stretches far beyond the horizon. The streets of Kutupalong are narrow, dusty and lined with tiny shacks made from black and orange tarpaulin. The muddy passageways climb 30 metres high before dropping down into small valleys where polluted and foul-smelling waters converge.

Laughter can occasionally be heard from dedicated tents where aid workers play games and sing songs with young refugee children. But Noor Kajol rarely visited these child-friendly spaces. Conservative gender roles meant her mother – now a widow – was prohibited from leaving the tent unaccompanied. Instead, her five children were required to perform daily chores like collecting firewood, water and aid.

Sometimes the children would forget where the distributions points were located, or misunderstand the instructions dealt by the aid workers. For days they would go hungry, waiting for the next opportunity to collect their rations. When darkness fell upon the camp, the whole family refused to leave their tent, no matter how desperately they needed the latrine. Decades of systematic violence at the hands of the Myanmar authorities meant domestic abuse was rife in the camps. For almost twelve hours, all six members of the family would confine themselves to those four plastic walls.

Mehedi returned to his software company but his thoughts were still in Cox's Bazar. He had been humbled by the small acts of kindness he had seen among the Rohingya – refugees who would give their last meagre rations to those showing more severe signs of hunger, and families who offered their small patch of earth to orphans in need of shelter. His clients had been understanding when he left during the first phase of the refugee influx, but with targets to hit and deadlines to meet, their patience was running out. Yet the work that had once excited Mehedi now seemed futile. Against their requests – and much to the concern of his friends who labelled him insane – Mehedi took a sabbatical from work and boarded another plane, destined for Cox's Bazar.

After some consultations with Rohingya leaders, Mehedi decided to invest the rest of his money in more dignified housing for refugees. He claimed a barren hill at one end of Kutupalong and transformed it into a brand new village – called Love Hill – with 55 bamboo homes. Shortly afterwards he received a donation from a friend and started building Love Hill 2. By the end of his sabbatical, Mehedi had built 140 homes for Rohingya refugees – enough to house over 500 people.

The design was not dissimilar to the houses that the Rohingya lived in at home. But under the Myanmar government, even the smallest home improvement required permission from the authorities – permission which was rarely granted. In Mehedi's village, the houses were to be painted sky blue with messages of hope graffitied on the walls – a display of both defiance and freedom.

Rohingya refugees flocked to the village to see the 'Banksy of Bangladesh' in action. Meanwhile, the sound of childish giggles and playful screams echoed between the vibrant walls as scores of young Rohingya made Love Hill their playground. Eventually, officials from the United Nations Refugee Agency (UNHCR) took notice, and asked Mehedi if they could house some of the most vulnerable Rohingya families in his two villages; among them, female-headed households like Noor Kajol's.

The detached homes – which are comfortable two-roomed structures – offer vulnerable families far greater privacy than the tarpaulin tents that choke the main Kutupalong refugee camp. Widows can roam the wide alleyways which are shared with other grieving women, and children can access the latrines, water pump and playground free from harassment.

But Love Hills 1 and 2 have been costly for Mehedi. As well as spending his entire savings on relief for the Rohingya, his software company has lost two clients. Despite this, he is already conjuring up his next project and later this year, he will find out whether he is the recipient of UNHCR's prestigious Nansen Refugee Award for outstanding service to the cause of refugees.

'Nothing compares to the feeling you get when you make someone else's life a little bit better. I know that what I do will not provide the Rohingya with a solution, but if I can help just one family then it is worth it.'

ABOUT KATIE

Katie Arnold is a freelance journalist and documentary producer who has worked with some of the biggest international broadcasters. She has spent the last three years covering human rights and humanitarian issues in Myanmar – with a particular focus on the Rohingya crisis – but has also reported from Bangladesh, Thailand, Kyrgyzstan, Morocco, the West Bank and the UK.

———

Find out more about Katie at:

W: www.katiearnold.co.uk
T: @kate_arno ♦ I: @kate_arno

18
WALKING ACROSS LAKE BAIKAL

Laura and Tim Moss spent a week walking across a frozen Siberian lake. Disaster hit when their stove stopped working, but a group of Russians gave them a new perspective on adventure

Laura and Tim Moss

As we lay swaddled in our tent, a loud rumbling noise echoed around us. For several seconds it seemed the world was collapsing beneath us, until a decisive cracking sound ended the show, and we breathed again.

We were suspended on a metre of ice, over the deepest part of the deepest lake in the world. It was −21°C outside, we were three days' walk from the nearest village and the lake had started to grumble at us. The straining ice was groaning beneath us and we had to trust it wasn't going to give way. Moreover, our stove had just broken. Father Baikal, as the lake is referred to by the local Russians, appeared to be irritated by our presence.

The stove was our lifeline. We relied on it to melt snow for water. Although we could eat the bread, salami and chocolate we had with us, with nothing to drink, life would soon become very difficult.

The ice was too thick for us to break through to the lake beneath and our efforts to melt snow in bottles in the sun during the day or in our sleeping bags at night hadn't been very successful. We lay in our sleeping bags, quietly wondering what to do.

The two of us have been on many adventures together since getting married six years ago. We've run ultramarathons and cycled around the world, crossed deserts on bike and foot, and wild camped in all conditions. As a married couple, we make excellent expedition partners, knowing each other's skills, strengths and limitations intimately. In times of stress – say, when a stove has broken in the middle of Siberia – we know what the other person will be feeling and understand instinctively how to avoid conflict which would make a difficult situation worse. For this reason, we chose to lie there in silence, listening only to the noise of the ice settling around us as the temperature dropped.

The plan for this expedition was to spend a week walking across frozen Lake Baikal, from west to east. We had been dropped off at the tip of an isolated peninsula halfway up the lake and planned to cross to the opposite shore and then back again in a large loop. We hoped to cover approximately 100 miles, carrying all our supplies and camping on the ice. We were expecting isolation, hardship and a physical challenge: in other words, the exact opposite of our office jobs back home.

We had spent much of our journey to Siberia casting our fellow Russian passengers as James Bond villains. Russians are usually portrayed as the bad guys in Western media so it was easy to allocate roles for the people we encountered as henchmen, assassins and spies. Even on the lake, we had set off at the same time as a group of three Russians who refused to return our smiles, thus confirming the stereotype. They were the only other people for miles around, and happened to be travelling across the lake in the same direction as us, but they clearly didn't want our company. We spent the first day on the ice passing each other with nothing more than a curt nod.

Towards the end of that first day, when we were gradually becoming used to the fact we were walking on ice, the Russians stopped ahead and waited for us to catch up. As we drew level, the bear-like man who appeared to be their leader gestured to a patch of flat ice nearby. He indicated that they were about to set up camp and that we might do the same. We were tired and ready to call it a day, so we shrugged and started setting up the tent. Although we were still not on speaking terms with our neighbours, it was hard to believe their intentions could be sinister out here.

The following morning, with no words having been exchanged, we decided to try to separate ourselves from the Russians. We were after the wilderness experience and had not expected to see anyone else on the ice, nor intended to follow in others' footsteps. This was about forging our own path, having our own adventure and learning how to cope with the extreme conditions in our own style. If we had wanted a guide, we would have found one. After coffee and porridge, we packed up the sledges and stomped off across the lake.

Travelling through snow is hard work. Although we occasionally found patches of bare ice, most of the lake's surface was covered in a thin layer of snow. This meant that dragging the sledges created a lot of friction, so it felt like constantly being pulled backwards. After a couple of hours, we found some old tyre tracks, where the snow was compacted and much firmer to walk on. The ice is thick enough in winter to support vehicles, meaning fishermen and tourists can drive across the lake, leaving tracks for skiers and walkers to follow.

The harder surface made the going much easier, but the Russians clearly had the same idea because at lunchtime they caught up with us again. We might have been the only people out there, but we were destined to keep meeting each other. As before, no smiles were returned, but the leader intimated a sign of thawing relations by handing us a piece of chocolate with a nod.

That evening, we decided to camp close to the Russians again. Despite our wish for isolation, it was comforting to know that they were nearby, in this most alien of environments. This was when disaster hit and the stove stopped working. We have used this stove hundreds of times, but nothing we tried could get it going. Tim sat down in the snow and took it apart piece by piece, replacing parts where we had spares and cleaning the rest, but the fuel pump still leaked and it didn't maintain enough pressure to operate. No stove meant no water, so it was a worrying turn of events.

After a couple of frustrating hours, both cold by then, we took a pan of snow over to the Russians' tent. They beckoned us in, put the pan on their kerosene heater and gave us a piece of *salo*, the cured pork that is a mainstay of the Siberian picnic. We discovered they were all academics from Novosibirsk and spoke basic English, so we talked about our planned journeys. They were planning to head north a few days later, diverging from our route. We went to bed with full water bottles, but still anxious about the days ahead. The loud noises coming from the lake did not help with this anxiety, as we lay in our sleeping bags wondering where our next drink would come from.

One of the features of camping at low temperatures is that every drop of moisture freezes, accumulating as ice on the inside of the tent. Every exhalation, every bead of sweat contributed to an indoor snow canopy and meant that any small movement sent down a shower of ice crystals. This explains why, when we heard the Russians out and about the following morning, we greeted them with a string of expletives as we sat up in our sleeping bags and were immediately covered in a deluge of ice. Despite the unconventional greeting, they offered to melt a pan of snow for us before they turned off their stove for the morning.

Their leader, Alex, said they were aiming to camp on a peninsula that evening, a finger of land that stuck out into the middle of the lake. If we joined them, we could build a campfire to melt snow for water that night then assess our options from there. Heading back the way we had come would have been tough going without the ability to make water, so it seemed sensible to stick with the Russians for now.

After a couple of hours dragging the sledges, we were feeling the effects of dehydration. The pan of snow Alex had melted for us was enough for coffee but no more, and the thirst was really beginning to kick in. Up ahead of us, we could see a long dark line scarring the lake. As we approached it, we realised that Father Baikal was looking out for us after all. The scar was a lead – a crack in the ice that exposes the lake beneath. Although it had frozen over, the new ice was only a couple of centimetres thick, which meant we could break through and access fresh water.

When friends had asked us if we would be fishing through the ice, we'd told them that the last thing we would want to do when walking on the surface of a frozen lake was to smash a hole in it. However, sitting at the edge of the lead, smashing a hole in the ice was exactly what we needed to do.

Along with all the specialist lightweight camping equipment, we were also carrying a heavy metal hammer picked up from a hardware store in Irkutsk. We needed it to bang in the ice screws necessary for pitching our tent on ice, but it probably weighed as much as the tent itself so it was nice to find another use for it. After a few swings, a spray of fresh water indicated we had punctured the lake's skin. We filled our water bottles, relieved, and treated ourselves to cold porridge – the breakfast we'd missed without water.

By mid-afternoon we had reached the edge of the peninsula, where we waited for the Russians. Alex had camped there before so he took us to a good spot he knew with an area cleared for a fire and a wall built from snow blocks to shelter a tent from the wind. Watching Laura haul her heavy sledge up the steep snow bank where the lake met land, Alex exclaimed 'She is Russian woman!' Coming from a burly Siberian, this was high praise.

We collected wood from the surrounding area and built a campfire, while Alex strung up a wire from which to hang cooking pots. We declined the offer to spend the night in their large tent, but gladly accepted the offer of meat stew for dinner. After we'd eaten, the Russians produced a battered plastic bottle of spirit – apparently cognac – and there followed a series of toasts: to international friendship, to 'British heroes' (us), to 'Russian heroes' (them) and above all to Lake Baikal. We spent several hours around the campfire that night discussing everything from our views on Brexit to their memories of the large group outdoor activities that used to be encouraged by the socialist state.

The following morning we woke to a cry of 'British heroes, breakfast ready!' as our unexpected hosts had risen early and prepared another stew. By this time we had devised a plan for continuing on our own: we would load our sledges with firewood which we could use to build a campfire again that evening and melt snow for water. That would allow us to reach the nearest town, two days' walk from where we were. Although we were nervous about starting a fire on the surface of our icy platform, we'd seen it done on a YouTube clip back at home and the Russians seemed unperturbed by the idea.

It was time to say goodbye to our new friends and we pressed chocolate bars into their hands as a way of saying a small thank you for all of their help.

We had to work hard over the next two days as we knew we only had enough wood for one night's camping and we still had a lot of miles to cover before we reached civilisation. We established a disciplined routine of walking for two hours before breaking for ten minutes, and repeated it until the sun went down.

Keeping the fire going that evening required all of Laura's concentration, because the heat of the blaze melted the ice beneath it, which in turn doused the flames. However, we managed to melt enough snow for dinner and drinks the next day, even if the result was that everything smelled like woodsmoke for the rest of the trip.

We were tired by the time we reached the town the following evening after another day of marching. We wandered the streets aimlessly in search of accommodation for the night before hesitantly approaching a group of surly-looking fishermen in military fatigues. Hearing our story, and the fact that we were English, they immediately broke into big grins and made us pose for a series of group photographs before they drove us to somewhere we could stay. We revelled in the warmth of our host's *banya* and slept soundly in a proper bed, safe in the knowledge that water was now available on tap and there was no risk of drowning in our sleep. We had survived Lake Baikal.

We had come to Siberia to get away from it all. We didn't want, nor had we expected, company out on the ice, but our experience was all the richer for it. We wanted isolated wilderness, but discovered that the joy of travelling is in the people you meet – in this case, our Russian heroes.

ABOUT LAURA AND TIM

Laura and Tim Moss firmly believe in the value that adventure can bring to everyday life. They have crossed the Wahiba Sands desert in Oman on foot, run the length of every Underground line in London, walked across Patagonia and, more recently, spent 16 months cycling around the world. Now back in normal employment, but with a better appreciation of a decent saddle, they spend their free time running The Next Challenge website, organising the Cycle Touring Festival and being involved with The Adventure Syndicate. They also offer The Next Challenge Grant, which funds people to go on adventures of their own.

Find out more about Laura and Tim at:

W: www.thenextchallenge.org

T: @lauralikeswater and @NextChallenge

I: @nextchallenge ✦ F: @thenextchallenge

19

STRANGERS IN THE HOLY LAND

To walk is to meet people on their level, face-to-face and shoulder to shoulder, and it serves more powerfully than anything else that I have found to highlight a shared humanity among all. Here are a few things I've come to think about and experience through my own journeys on foot

Leon McCarron

As humans, we are designed to move at three miles an hour. I am not an evolutionary biologist, but I know this to be true. (I read it in a newspaper article about evolutionary biology.)

Now, in the age of immediacy in everything from news to transportation, to choose to move at this speed – in other words, to walk – for an entire day, or for a week or a year, might seem unusual. It should not be. We've been doing this for 60,000 years: walking is our natural rhythm. To walk for any length of time forces us into a slowness of movement, thought and relationships and, in the twenty-first century, it has the added benefit of allowing us to draw connections between people and places and ideas that would otherwise be lost in our helter-skelter world.

Since the summer of 2012 I have travelled over 6,000 miles on foot. The journeys upon which these footfalls – 20 million of them – have taken place have been varied in location, theme and outcome, and as such I've struggled to find adequate terminology to describe them; expedition seems too grand, adventure too vague. I have settled for now on simply calling them, unhelpfully, 'long journeys' – a turn of phrase that has yet to catch on.

These long journeys have made my feet and legs initially painful, then ultimately stronger. My heart too is undoubtedly in much better shape than it was when I began, but most interesting of all is what happens externally when I walk. I am able to observe places and details that I wouldn't otherwise see, freed as I am from the constrictive ribbons of tarmac that slice across our landscapes, and I meet people whose paths I can only cross because I am on foot. The stories that I hear, and am then part of, in these instances are what make walking journeys so unique and immersive; I sometimes think that I could draw maps of where I've been based not on geographical features but on interaction, conversation and hospitality.

In 2015 I set off to walk a loop of the Holy Land, from Jerusalem to Mount Sinai. Over the course of five months and 1,000 miles I walked through the verdant green hills of the West Bank, down the rocky spine of Jordan and then out across the vast deserts and granite peaks of Sinai. It was a journey that utilised pioneering new hiking trails in the region; trails that themselves had grown out of well-used, centuries-old Bedouin paths and, before that, from the pilgrimage routes that criss-crossed the land between religious centres. Even these were recycled, having developed atop the trading thoroughfares that connected the ancient empires of East to West and, originally, from the paths blazed by our adventurous ancestors as they strode out of Africa.

I wanted to use the trails to see another side of the Middle East, and of the region at the heart of some of the most intractable geopolitical problems of our time. I hoped that these layers of history underneath my feet would help as I walked, and what I found, overwhelmingly, was a landscape where the noise of the contemporary divisions has overshadowed the fundamental truth of the Holy Land; that it is still a place where kindness and hospitality span the voids created by religious and ethnic detachment.

Near the town of Jericho, not long after I set off, I stayed in a refugee camp with a woman called Umm Huda. She ran a women's cooperative and found a place for me to sleep, then fed me until I nearly burst, saying, 'What would your mother say if she knew you weren't eating enough? Have more chicken!' In the morning she knocked on the door to tell me that she'd made sure there was hot water for me to bathe with; this in a town where running water is unreliable at best for residents, and the idea of heated showers a rare luxury. My gushing thanks were dismissed with a slight blush: 'You're a guest here. I wouldn't have it any other way.'

Farther north in the West Bank, a young shopkeeper called Amir – a bear of a man with a huge, silky beard – saw me walking past and rushed out of his doorway to wrap me in a hug so tight that my sunglasses popped off. 'Come in!' he shouted. 'You must let me make you some lunch.' Later he took me to his mosque, just to make sure I knew how peaceful Islam was. 'See?' he said inside the ornate doorway where rows of sandals lay discarded, awaiting the return of their praying owners. 'It's just like a church. Why would people be scared of this?' The next day, in a church in the next town, I had a remarkably similar experience and I told my Christian host, George, that it reminded me of Amir and the mosque. 'Of course it does,' he said. 'Kindness should not change based on religion.'

These small acts of generosity towards a traveller apparently in need became the rule rather than the exception. Once or twice a day in the West Bank I would be ushered into the home of a stranger and a cup of sweet black tea would be pressed into my hand. Food would usually follow; often huge platters of eggs and hummus and olives and tomatoes and *za'atar* spice, all gloriously fresh and local, and delicious.

This trend of regular, uninhibited hospitality then continued, I was happy to note, as I passed into Jordan and onwards towards Sinai. Kindness does not stop at checkpoints and borders. In the verdant green hills of Ajloun in northern Jordan I would sit with Bedouin, watching their flocks of sheep roam the hillside, and we'd share viscous black coffee and thick *labneh* bread, baked fresh in the ashes of the fire. 'Why did you invite me to eat with you?' I would sometimes ask. The replies varied: 'Because you're a guest', 'Because I wanted to know where you're from', 'Because you looked hungry and tired', 'Because it is an excuse for me to drink more tea, and I am addicted to the sugar.'

I used to worry that, with such intense regularity of experience, I might become complacent or simply begin to expect to be looked after, but kindnesses are not memories that wear thin. We remember them long after the other details of a chance meeting are gone. This too is something to be grateful for. The story that I recall most fondly from my journey in the Holy Land came from a man called Mahmoud outside the city of Kerak. I had just emerged from the third and final of the 'great wadis', vast canyons that cut across Jordan, each at least 800 metres deep. The sun had fallen like timber beyond a jagged horizon and the last light of day exploded laterally across the sky, illuminating for a final brief moment a small country road along the plateau. Two small houses flanked my progress and, outside one, a small and compact man wearing a fine broad moustache watched me advance. '*Ta-al*,' he said quietly, instructing rather than asking: 'Come,' and, taking me by the hand, he led me into his front room. 'You must be very tired. I wonder if you would permit my sons and I to wash your feet? Afterwards, perhaps we can eat dinner together.' The biblical scale of his gesture was not lost on me and it was all I could do not to burst into tears.

Even when my boots were removed and the toxic stench of month-old socks revealed, the offer was not rescinded and cool water was poured over my soft, fleshy feet. Later, over a dinner of *maklouba*, where chicken and rice are cooked together and then served by upending the pot like a sandcastle, I asked Mahmoud what he first thought when he saw me. 'I already told you,' he said. 'I thought you must be tired.'

'But did you not wonder what I was doing?' I persisted.

'That was not my business. There is time for that once you are rested and fed.'

The remains of dinner were pressed into a box and set beside my bag as Mahmoud's sons prepared me a bed for the night. I tried to refuse the food – there was enough to feed his family for at least another day and I knew he was not a wealthy man, but he brushed me off once more.

Later, another generous stranger summed up both Mahmoud's kindness and many of the other experiences I had of unsolicited hospitality. 'In Islam we have a saying,' he told me. 'Give without remembering, and take without forgetting. This is how I live.'

In a region from which it seems we now hear only stories of conflict and despair, why is it that I was treated so well? A friend in Jerusalem thought the answer simple. He attributed it to the story of Abraham, or Ibrahim, the patriarch to over half of humanity and the original backpacker in the Middle East. In the desert, he said, Abraham's tent was left open at all four corners so that travellers from every direction would know they were welcome to take shelter. That spirit of openness and kindness that Abraham represented, said my friend, as borne out through scriptural and oral traditions, has filtered down through the generations to his descendants. It should therefore be no surprise that hospitality is still prevalent.

Perhaps this is true. If we take the Abrahamic inheritance out of the question for a moment, however, why else do people react like this? And is it something that is restricted simply to a sacred landscape? Of course, it is not. I have found the same thing everywhere that I have been. In the USA, on the first day of a long journey when I was still fresh and scared and undoubtedly lost, an elderly man in a New York Knicks cap gave me a twenty-dollar bill and paid for my breakfast at the diner where we met. 'Use that money to have an adventure,' he said, 'and when you're done, head back home and get a good job.' I fulfilled half of the deal, at least. In Patagonia, when I rode a horse across Argentina and made use of hooves rather than feet, I was brought into the remote *estancias* that dot the wastes of the southern steppe. As in the Middle East, food and drink were served first, and questions asked only later once it was clear that I was rested and satiated (a notable difference, however, was that the tea and chicken of the Holy Land were replaced with Argentinian wine and steak – both options have their merits).

I have found the same sense of hospitality in Spain when walking the Camino de Santiago, in Rwanda, in New Zealand, in Vietnam. In China a man I'd never met invited me to spend Chinese New Year with him and his confused but gracious family. In a Mongolian winter two nomads brought me out of the blizzards in the Gobi Desert to serve me a local delicacy of boiled goat's intestines wrapped inside more boiled goat's intestines.

During a six-week journey in Iran I used my tent only once because every village I passed through had at least one person who insisted that I sleep in their home. I consider it the greatest privilege of my life to have seen so much of the world, and to have that experience accompanied by these spontaneous, consistent acts of kindness. Whenever there have been people around I have never gone hungry, nor ever stayed lost. I have only ever been refused water once in my life, and that was in Wales (and, admittedly, that in itself was an anomaly in the midst of an otherwise wonderfully welcoming bike tour).

Here's what I think. The kindness that is shown from strangers, to strangers, is something that is in our DNA. As well as not being an evolutionary biologist, I am also not a geneticist, so perhaps take that statement in the metaphorical way in which it is intended. I am, however, a walker, and a professional stranger, and I have found kindness everywhere.

Hospitality is not location-dependent. It is, rather, an innate response to seeing someone vulnerable or in need. Everyone who has looked after me as I've walked has done so, as far as I can tell, because they want to. It does not seem to be an obligation, which would make it something else entirely. That said, however, this is probably a good point at which to note a few other factors that inform my experience and the response that I receive. I am white. I am a male. I travel with a British passport (and an Irish passport) and I wear Western clothing. My gear is expensive by most standards around the world and, no matter how dishevelled I look nor how bad I smell, it is immediately obvious to most that I meet that I am travelling out of choice. That is to say, the joys and hardships that I face are self-inflicted. I have decided to put myself in uncomfortable or unusual situations.

It is inconceivable that these things would not affect how I am treated. I attribute much of the intimacy of my journeys to the act of walking, but it's true too that I take those steps with an imbued privilege. This is an unfair advantage that I have done nothing to earn; in the lottery of life, I happened to luck out. I cannot say what experiences I would have had if any of my characteristics changed, but it is likely that some – perhaps many – would have been different. My perspective, therefore, is skewed, but for what it's worth, here's what I've concluded.

There is now an increasing fear of the stranger. The idea of 'otherness' being a bad thing, or something to be afraid of, is growing. We see this, as I write, through recent political upheavals in the UK and the USA, and under the dark cloud of rising populism across Europe. That fear of 'the other' grows, primarily, through the mass media; through the misrepresentation that the world we live in is riven with perpetual conflicts, and that it is an inherently dangerous place. This is nonsense. Up close, at ground level, through first-hand experiences, I have found that as a species we are much more similar than we are different. There are fears and biases, of course, but there is still an intrinsic goodness among people and no matter what it is that divides us, that which unites us is much stronger. In the absence of any religious beliefs in my life, this notion is perhaps the bedrock of my personal philosophy. It's worth repeating: despite everything that we might hear about the wars and atrocities and despair – which do exist of course, but do not define us – people are fundamentally good. One of the frontiers of modern-day travel and exploration then, to my mind, is the attempt to combat this notion that we live in a broken world, and we can do this by celebrating our diversity and cultural heritage.

Here, then, is my challenge to you, the reader. Go out into the world. Go to the places that you would normally visit and also to those that you would not. Spend time with people. If you can, walk, and if you do walk, be sure that you are walking to listen. Absorb the stories you hear and perhaps share some of your own. Then, when all is said and done and the trail beneath your feet has run out, return home and share what you have learned. We live in the digital age, and we can disseminate the findings of our explorations with greater ease – and to a larger audience – than ever before. Let's remember too that the negativity – that of the evil world, full of bad people – will be spreading just as fast, so we do this not just for personal indulgence nor self-gratification. We do this to push the narrative of a good world. The world that I live in is one in which the majority of strangers share the same basic hopes and dreams, and go out of their way to show kindness to anyone that may pass by their tent or house, along road or trail. I hope that's the world you find too and, if so, I can't wait to hear about it.

ABOUT LEON

Leon McCarron is a Northern Irish writer and film-maker specialising in long-distance, human-powered journeys. He has cycled from New York to Hong Kong, walked 3,000 miles across China, trekked 1,000 miles through the Empty Quarter desert and travelled along Iran's longest river by a variety of human-powered methods. His most recent trips have been following the Santa Cruz River in Patagonia on horseback and walking from Jerusalem to Mount Sinai.

————

Find out more about Leon at:

W: www.leonmccarron.com ◆ T: @leonmccarron
I: @leonmccarron ◆ F: @leonmccarron

20
LOVE
TRUMPS
HATE

A journey through the land
of the free and the fearful

Lilly Quinn and Sarah Little

In some way, we always knew our trip would involve the kindness of strangers.

Whilst we were careful to ensure we had the fallback of a tent to sleep in, had the resilience to wait for the next ride, had some form of food in our pack... ultimately, we were couch-surfing, hitch-hiking and volunteering for food on a penniless trip across America. We were depending on people – on strangers – to help us progress each day, whether through a ride or a place to sleep or with the leftover food they no longer wanted to eat. If anything, this was the reason for our trip: we wanted to push ourselves to meet people we would never have any other reason to meet. To swap stories and experiences with strangers whose lives would never otherwise have crossed ours. By the end of 48 states and five months, we were blown away by how many times we experienced the kindness of strangers.

One particular story came about in South Dakota: a 'flyover state' by many standards. We'd been told plenty of times that there was nothing to see in South Dakota, and that we were better off rushing through because – especially in the north – there was 'no sense of kindness amongst folk' and only a 'coldness' to be found. Despite this, we wanted to see Mount Rushmore in Rapid City, so we stuck out our thumbs. Arriving in a truck late in the night, we slept in the cab and set off up the road around 7 a.m., the early summer sun already hot enough to spark a sweat. With the main highway still a way off, hazy in the distance, we hauled our heavy packs up the side of the road, straddling the jagged line where the tarmac broke off into scrubby grass, fearful of getting too close to the vehicles on a route with no sidewalk. Up ahead, a car swerved off the road partly at the exit but mostly on to the hard shoulder. The car was unremarkable for mid-America, but we noticed two bumper stickers on the back. One was the classic *Coexist*, written using a mixture of different religious symbols. The other, in pride of place, stated simply: *You can't take my guns*. This could be interesting. A woman clambered out of the driver's side, already talking at us despite the fact we were still some distance away.

'Where are you going? And at this time! In this heat! With those big packs! What are you doing out here?!'

We laughed, unsure why this kind-faced woman was so flabbergasted by our presence. We explained our story, and she offered to take us to Mount Rushmore (she lived over that way) if we helped unload her shopping. Amazing! Deal. Over the course of the early morning's conversation we discovered in Angie a woman who was, like many, battered and bruised from a life less than fair, but someone who embraced that turmoil as a reminder of what is better out there: how important it is to love and to believe in love. Here was a woman who embodied the phrase 'what doesn't kill you makes you stronger' and welcomed us into her life wholeheartedly, despite knowing nothing about us beyond an hour's conversation. After unloading the shopping at Angie's house – a beautiful ranch in the heart of the Black Hills that she had hand-built with her late husband – she dropped us at Mount Rushmore and asked us if we would like to be picked up by her afterwards and to spend the night at her ranch. We hesitated, knowing we had been aiming to reach an ecovillage that was still 600 miles away by the next day, but at the same time a gut instinct told us that Angie was someone we wanted to spend more time getting to know. We said yes.

After an underwhelming couple of hours at Mount Rushmore – who knew carving faces into otherwise beautiful rock and surrounding it with concrete and gravelled pathways could be so ugly, aye?! – Angie picked us up and began the drive back to her ranch.

'If you were doing this trip with money, what would you do around here that you've missed out on?'

We didn't hesitate to answer – the Badlands. The Badlands of South Dakota are a nature lover's dream: acres of valleys and towers of rock, carved by water over millions of years, leaving a dramatic moonscape favoured by cowboy films. We'd been desperate to go after skirting it in a truck on the way to Rapid City, but resigned ourselves to the fact it would still be there for a future trip. Angie pulled into a gas station.

'I'm going to fill my car with gas. You drive me home and pick up some drinks and snacks, then go off to the Badlands for the afternoon. Text me on your way home and I'll put dinner on.'

We couldn't believe what we were hearing. We had known this woman for roughly five hours and here she was, giving us her car for the day to go explore. Here she was, trusting us to come back with it, and showing such open-hearted kindness it was hard to know what to say beyond an excited jumble of 'thank you's and 'oh my god's. We spent an incredible day at the Badlands before driving back to Angie's, sharing more stories and learning more about America, sitting out on her porch drinking hard lemonade and watching the lightning roll in over the Black Hills: an end to a day we could never have imagined at seven that morning on the side of the road.

At the end of the day, the kindness of strangers comes down to trust. When you're penniless, pretend or otherwise, you're in a position where you have no choice but to trust in others. If you need to get somewhere or do something, you have no other choice but to open your arms and your mind and see who comes along to help, and what you can do for them in return. And putting control in the hands of strangers takes a massive leap of faith – whether you're offering the help or receiving it.

As children we are taught not to trust strangers. That works as a simple guideline for minors, but what happens when we grow up? We're never told to stop not trusting in strangers. We're not taught to trust our gut instead and to realise that, for the most part, people are good. So many of us aren't ever encouraged to have an open mind and to travel the world, experiencing different cultures and meeting new people. In fact, it seemed to us that American people are encouraged – by their culture, by the news, by the people around them – not to leave the country at all.

'Why would you want to leave America? We have everything you need right here!'

'Don't get on an airplane – you might get blown up or it might crash!'

'Getting a passport is difficult and expensive.'

There are too many reasons to stay, and no experience of what's out there to convince them to leave. A culture built on the desire for freedom, for the American Dream, has in so many instances turned into a fear of the outside. Fear controls and fear sells. The media is a huge part of this cycle, telling tales of violence, hatred and anger. But these tales are abstracted;

they are of some 'other' place, some 'other' person, and are taken out of any human context. We're taught to walk the planet wondering, for every stranger we meet, not about who they are with any understanding, but whether or not they could be 'that bad person from the news'; assuming the worst, and believing we should protect ourselves.

We will forever remember the feeling of trepidation on setting off for our first day hitch-hiking in the USA. We had been volunteering with a food rescue organisation in Boston the day before and they couldn't believe what we were about to do. They told us that 'America is different' and 'Forty per cent of people in Maine [where we were next heading] are on meth', and that we didn't understand the country. We were paraded around the group to be told by everyone how dangerous it is to hitch in America, and that we would never make it alive. We were shocked that a group of people who were seemingly very open-minded had such a narrow, negative view of their country. Worse is that we started to believe it. We began to question what we were doing.

'Is America different? Are we being naive?'

The scary thing is how quickly and easily that fear spreads – it's contagious. We had gone from two strong-minded women who had hitch-hiked around the world without fear, to two women questioning whether what we were doing was safe in this country that we'd apparently underestimated.

After a stirring of concern, and a farewell comprised of 'Have you even heard of the Craigslist killer? No? Google him', we trusted we were doing the right thing and took the steps to start hitching. Before we'd even put our packs down at that first hitch stop we were picked up by three lovely lads who took us all the way to Portland, Maine, and even put us up for the night!

Trust in humanity: affirmed. Whilst it was sad that fear had got the better of the food project team, what was wonderful was how often kindness triumphed over fear.

But people often did have to fight what has been so internalised. It was a battle to choose to trust us – to trust strangers – and we witnessed the struggle happening behind their eyes. They wanted to help but everything they'd learned told them that it's dangerous to help a stranger, that hitch-hikers are murderers, that strangers may cause harm. 'But they don't look dangerous? And what happens if I read on the news that something has happened to these ladies and I didn't help?' For us, that choice to help us despite the voices crying danger in their minds was a true show of kindness. We'll never forget the mother and daughter who pulled over as far away from us as they could whilst still being able to be heard, and called out of the car, 'You're not going to murder us, are you?' before agreeing to take us with them on their journey. We spent two days travelling with this incredible duo, and they said to us that we had made their trip (not before confessing that they had only initially pulled over to give us a Gatorade, but that the fear of 'someone else picking us up and killing us' got the better of them).

That was something that we found particularly curious. That often people helped us in order to 'save us' from all the 'bad people'. We learned quickly that the majority of people believe they are the only kind ones out there. It was a beautiful part of this trip to not only warm our own hearts with the kindness of strangers, and those at home who we passed stories on to, but also to spread that love around the hearts of Americans we met each day. To reassure each person, just by talking about our trip, that they weren't the only kind one out there and that they didn't have to be afraid. People were shocked and surprised that so many others had helped us and that we hadn't run into more trouble. One lady we hitched with said hearing our stories gave her 'hope in Americans and hope in humanity'. Some people did let the fear win but more often than not, kindness triumphed.

In life, we need to not let fear take the lead. We need to assume that strangers are kind first and foremost, and then to use our gut to determine anything further. We need to see humans as individuals and to fight the anger and hatred society and news encourage us to feel towards the 'other'. We're all strangers in the end, and we're worth so much more than the sum of our parts. All it takes is for you to make that decision to trust a stranger, and show a little kindness.

Throughout our five-month trip, we were welcomed into the lives of hundreds of ordinary people and shown kindnesses we could never have imagined, learning so much about what makes this vast, complicated, vulnerable country tick. People went above and beyond to not only show kindness by helping us, but by taking a genuine interest in what we wanted to achieve and allowing us a glimpse into their own lives. We learned that friendship, hope and kindness will always prevail if you let it. We learned that the kindness of strangers exists naturally, and that it is fear and learned behaviour from the news, the media and society that restrict it. We learned that you can't let someone else's experience define your own, and that we can become so blinded by labels and numbers that we forget about individual people.

What we ultimately learned is that love will always trump hate. We just have to let it.

ABOUT LILLY
AND SARAH

'Pretenniless' means 'pretend penniless'. In the 2016 election year, Lilly Quinn and Sarah Little spent 20 weeks hitch-hiking all 48 mainland states of the USA without spending a single cent on anything, from the moment they stepped off the plane. These days Lilly is continuing her travels in Australia, and Sarah works in video production. Every now and then they entertain the idea of a second trip in Japan...

Find out more about Lilly and Sarah at:

W: www.pretenniless.com
T: @pretenniless @SarahSmall
I: @pretenniless @LillyQuinny
F: @Pretenniless ♦ P: @pretenniless

21
KEEP ON TRUCKIN'

When Lindsey decided she didn't want to take a plane after one of the best adventures of her life, she didn't realise it would be sowing the seed for an entirely new adventure altogether...

Lindsey Cole

'Here you go, mate. I can't go any further than here,' said Darren, who was driving us along in a brand-new massive shiny red five-million-dollar crane. I jumped out and walked the 20 minutes down the dusty red Pilbara road to the retirement home where I was visiting a 93-year-old Aboriginal lady called Daisy.

In the early 1900s the Australian government constructed a fence in Western Australia that ran the entire length of the state, coast to coast, to contain the exploding population of rabbits that white settlers had introduced. Around that time they also introduced a scheme which saw all mixed-race children taken away from their Aboriginal mothers to be raised by Christians throughout the country. The government deemed that they had a better chance in assimilating into white society this way, believing that the Aboriginal side would be bred out through two generations of enforced marriage to whites. Every mother of a part-Aboriginal child was aware that their offspring could be taken away from them at any time and they were powerless to stop the abductors. This happened throughout Australia for decades. The children who were forcibly taken from their families during this era became known as the Stolen Generation.

In 1931, Daisy and her sister Molly and cousin Gracie, were forcibly removed from their homes and placed in a settlement 1,000 miles away. They each had different itinerant fathers who'd worked on the rabbit-proof fence.

Barnes & Noble Booksellers #2607
300 Andover Park W Ste 200
Tukwila, WA 98188
206-575-3965

STR:2607 REG:001 TRN:6801 CSHR:Victoria W

Kindness of Strangers: Travel Stories Th
  9781786855312   T1
  (1 @ 13.99)   13.99

Subtotal   13.99
Sales Tax T1 (10.100%)   1.41
TOTAL   15.40
VISA   15.40
  Card#: XXXXXXXXXXXX5438
  Expdate: XX/XX
  Auth: 09785D
  Entry Method: Chip Read

  Application Label: CHASE VISA
  AID: a0000000031010
  TVR: 0080008000
  TSI: e800

A MEMBER WOULD HAVE SAVED   1.40

Connect with us on Social

Facebook- @BNSouthcenter
Instagram- @bn_southcenter
Twitter-   @BNSouthcenter

055.01C   07/25/2021 03:06PM

CUSTOMER COPY

With a sales receipt or Barnes & Noble.com packing slip, a full refund in the original form of payment will be issued from any Barnes & Noble Booksellers store for returns of new and unread books, and unopened and undamaged music CDs, DVDs, vinyl records, electronics, toys/games and audio books made within 30 days of purchase from a Barnes & Noble Booksellers store or Barnes & Noble.com with the below exceptions:

Undamaged NOOKs purchased from any Barnes & Noble Booksellers store or from Barnes & Noble.com may be returned within 14 days when accompanied with a sales receipt or with a Barnes & Noble.com packing slip or may be exchanged within 30 days with a gift receipt.

A store credit for the purchase price will be issued (i) when a gift receipt is presented within 60 days of purchase, (ii) for all textbooks returns and exchanges, or (iii) when the original tender is PayPal.

Items purchased as part of a Buy One Get One or Buy Two, Get Third Free offer are available for exchange only, unless all items purchased as part of the offer are returned, in which case such items are available for a refund (in 30 days). Exchanges of the items sold at no cost are available only for items of equal or lesser value than the original cost of such item.

Opened music CDs, DVDs, vinyl records, electronics, toys/games, and audio books may not be returned, and can be exchanged only for the same product and only if defective. NOOKs purchased from other retailers or sellers are returnable only to the retailer or seller from which they were purchased pursuant to such retailer's or seller's return policy. Magazines, newspapers, eBooks, digital downloads, and used books are not returnable or exchangeable. Defective NOOKs may be exchanged at the store in accordance with the applicable warranty.

Returns or exchanges will not be permitted (i) after 30 days or without receipt or (ii) for product not carried by Barnes & Noble.com, (iii) for purchases made with a check less than 7 days prior to the date of return.

Policy on receipt may appear in two sections.

Return Policy

With a sales receipt or Barnes & Noble.com packing slip, a full refund in the original form of payment will be issued from any Barnes & Noble Booksellers store for returns of new and unread books, and unopened and undamaged music CDs, DVDs, vinyl records, electronics, toys/games and audio books made within 30 days of purchase from a Barnes & Noble Booksellers store or Barnes & Noble.com with the below exceptions:

Once at the Moore River Native Settlement, near Perth, the girls weren't allowed to speak their native language; they had to speak English. They weren't given bed sheets unless VIPs visited and they were said to have lived in squalor. Daisy's older sister, Molly, didn't like it at the settlement. She wanted to be home with her mother, like any 14-year-old would. So, she engineered an escape along with Daisy and Gracie and they ran all the way home, 1,000 miles to Jigalong, following the rabbit-proof fence. They had no shoes, no provisions and no shelter but they made it home in spite of being tracked by police.

In 2007, my father passed away suddenly whilst I was backpacking in Australia. A few months beforehand I had read a book called *Follow the Rabbit-Proof Fence*, which documented Daisy, Molly and Gracie's story, and for some reason these girls brought me solace when I was at the lowest point in my life. So I vowed I would return to pay homage to their journey. It took me nine years to pluck up the courage to head back. I didn't know if the fence was still there. I didn't know if it would be physically possible to retrace their journey. And I didn't know if it would be deemed culturally insensitive for me to do so; the girls' strength and characters had helped me through a dark time, but I was fully aware that their story was sensitive. So I bought a one-way ticket to Perth to find my answers, decided if it did get too difficult that I would pull out, and I located Daisy's daughters and asked for their blessing to retrace their mother's journey.

———

My heart was swollen with pure delight, and my self-esteem could challenge that of my cartoon hero, She-Ra. It was the best thing I'd ever done. For 1,000 miles I had walked alone through wild bush, salt lakes and desert. My only companion was my walking trolley that contained everything I needed for my journey. I named him Trevor, after my dad.

After ten weeks I walked into Jigalong, a community which crests on the edge of the Little Sandy Desert, from which Molly, Daisy and Gracie had been forcibly removed and where the rabbit-proof fence which led them home passes through. Molly's daughter, Maria, joined me for the last five kilometres and took me into her home for the week. I would sit on her veranda with her as she would tell me stories about her mother.

Molly passed away in 2004. Gracie never made it back to Jigalong – she'd heard that her mother was in a town called Wiluna so left the girls halfway along the fence. But I had heard that Daisy was still alive. As I was so close, I wanted to meet her to tell her how her and her sisters had inspired me. There was no public transport so I hitched.

I told Darren, the truckie who gave me the lift, about my story, the rabbit-proof fence story and that I was about to meet Daisy herself.

'Good luck, mate,' said Darren, as I closed the door on his truck.

Daisy's grandson greeted me when I arrived and guided me down the hallway of the retirement home. And there she was, this little old lady lying there quietly, who 85 years beforehand had trekked 1,000 miles to get home to her family. On her windowsill stood a framed image of the book that was in my bag and that I had read just before I lost my dad. I sat beside her and held her hand as her grandson told her why I was there.

After I met Daisy, I sat on a kerb and found myself in a state of euphoria. It had taken me ten weeks to retrace her journey to walk the rabbit-proof fence into Jigalong. I couldn't bring myself to fly back to Perth in just 60 minutes. It had seemed easy enough hitching from Jigalong to meet Daisy, so I decided to hitch back.

I stood beside Trevor, on the side of the main road, holding a sign that read: *Perth*. Within five minutes a ute pulled up. Out stepped a construction worker whose belly poked through the bottom of his shirt, his eyes magnified behind his thick-rimmed glasses. He didn't have a single hair on the top of his head, which shined like a polished cricket ball in the 38-degree, blazing desert sun. Mark was heading to his work campsite three hours south, so I hopped in.

The next service station was only two hours away, and I planned to get another lift from there, but Mark insisted he take me as far as he was going – to his campsite.

'There's a pool and as much food as you want. For free.' He turned to look at me, like I was a hobo who must be frothing at the mouth over the thought of free food.

'Thanks, but it would be great if you dropped me at the service station,' I replied.

'Only problem is,' he said, as beads of sweat drizzled down his bald head like the yolk on a cracked boiled egg, 'guests aren't allowed to stay, so you'll have to stay in my room.' If his proposal of free food and the pool hadn't worked, he was certainly not going to entice me with the offer of sharing his room.

I declined again.

'Suit yourself.' He paused, and then pressed again. 'So, you don't want as much food as you want for free?'

I'd just spent two and a half months in the middle of nowhere on rations. I thought I could survive on the bag of crisps I had in Trevor. I shook my head and told him the service station would be fine. He was beginning to creep me out.

Halfway through the journey we passed Karajini National Park, which boasts ancient cavernous gorges, cascading waterfalls and crystal-clear waterways. I'd been told it was worth a visit, but I just wanted to get back to Perth so I could bask in my achievements of walking the rabbit-proof fence and meeting Daisy.

'What, so you don't want to go to one of the most beautiful places in the world?' Mark said, when I declined his offer of a detour to the park. 'You don't want to bomb into the pools in your underwear?'

My creep-dar was raging red. He had just mentioned my underwear. There was no way he was going to see me in mine, nor did I have any interest in seeing him in his with his pokey-out belly hanging over his Y-fronts.

'Suit yourself,' he said again.

To my relief, Mark dropped me off at the Oskie service station as I'd requested. He insisted on waiting with me until I found my next lift.

A young lad pulled in to fill up his battered Fiesta, which was laden with his life's belongings. He looked like he was going a long way.

'Are you going to Perth by any chance?' I called out.

He looked up, as the nozzle was indulging his car with its next energy load. He was wearing a cap back to front and an oversized basketball top.

'Yeh, but I'm staying in Newman tonight, in a cheap motel.'

Perfect, I thought. I knew people in Newman, so I would have a place to crash. I grabbed Trevor and legged it to the Fiesta, managing to evade a sweaty embrace with Mark.

As we set off, Tim told me that Broome's pizza lovers were going to be most distressed by his departure. He had been in

Broome for college and worked in the pizza shop to support his studies. But he hadn't been to any lectures since he arrived so decided after a year of partying it was probably time to leave.

'Yeh, man. I don't know what they're going to do without me. I *am* the pizza guy,' he bragged. 'I used to chop up all the veg and shit.' I didn't want to break it to him, but I assumed they'd find someone relatively easily. Tim was 18, and I was under the impression he hadn't hung out with many girls before.

'So...' he said, tilting his sunglasses, peering over them at me, 'do you know any famous people?'

Famous people? Why would I know any famous people? I thought. 'Er, no. Do you?' I politely responded.

'Yeh,' he boasted, with a massive cheesy grin taking over his sunburned face. 'I've met a couple of prime ministers.' He hesitated as he waited for a response from me.

'Oh, right.'

'Yeh, my mum works in government, so I meet prime ministers whenever I want. I'm always stoned too.' He chuckled to himself. There wasn't an atom inside me that believed him, perhaps because he also mentioned that the only time he'd ever left the state was to go to Wet 'n' Wild, a theme park in Queensland.

He asked me what I was doing out here so I told him about the rabbit-proof fence.

'Do you know the story?' I asked.

'Nah.' He dismissed me, not taking in anything I'd just said. I wasn't surprised, considering what I'd seen of Tim already, but it saddened me that he wasn't interested in his country's history.

Tim held his phone in one hand, resting it on the wheel as he dialled a number with his other hand, using just his elbow to steer. 'I'll just call the motel so they don't run out of rooms.'

I nodded, and looked out of the window, taking in the scenery of where I'd been walking.

'Hold on,' Tim said down the phone. Then he said to me, 'You don't mind sharing a queen-sized bed, do you?'

I didn't answer – I think the reaction on my face was enough of a response.

'So, how old are you?' he asked, having finished booking his night's accommodation, which I would not be sharing with him. 'Or should I not ask a *lady*?' he said, again tilting his sunglasses, this time giving me a creepy wink.

'Thirty-three,' I answered.

His eyes bulged from behind his sunnies and his mouth gaped wide open. He almost choked with shock. 'I didn't think you were *that* old.'

When Tim realised I was out of his age threshold and that our futures probably wouldn't align, he began to rap, drumming his hands on the steering wheel. He then told me about a time he sang with a famous rapper live on stage to 10,000 people, when he was eight years old. 'Yeh, man, he saw me singing and just picked me out of the crowd. He said, "Get that little kid up here."'

Thankfully, his passenger wing mirror had had a previous bust-up with another vehicle sometime before, so he didn't see as I turned my head out of the window and silently howled with laughter. I wanted to have a clipboard to note down all the errors in his terrible chat to give him feedback for the future. Despite the fact he was driving all the way down to Perth, I decided to part ways with Tim in Newman and try a new lift the next day. Two hours with his bad chat was arduous enough. I couldn't handle another two days.

The next morning I stood at the service station just outside Newman, again with my sign for Perth. It's sort of hit-and-miss with random vehicles; I didn't get a good vibe from either Mark or Tim. So this time I thought I'd try my luck with trucks. Trucks are expected to be somewhere. They're working. They're tracked. So I deemed them a safer option. The Great Northern Highway is a busy route for trucks due to the amount of mining. Whenever the drivers came into the service station to pay I'd approach them and tell them my story. Some would apologise because they weren't able to give me a lift, and others almost ran away when they saw me approach them. Many companies don't allow their drivers to pick up passengers as if anything happened they're not covered for insurance.

A guy wearing a navy sleeveless vest with white salt sweat stains on the chest was opening his bottle of chocolate milk as he came out of the service station.

'Are you heading south?' I asked. He nodded.

I told him what I'd done and why I wanted a lift. I didn't want to appear like a tight, thrifty backpacker; I wanted him to know I just couldn't bring myself to fly because I'd walked the rabbit-proof fence.

He chuckled, took a swig of his chocolate milk, looked at his truck to contemplate his decision as he wiped his mouth with his hand and then nodded. Hurrah.

I had assumed that truckies were chauvinistic, racist and potty-mouthed characters. Dave would prove me wrong. He was sweet, caring and a real gent. I broke the ice by telling him about the 18-year-old ex-pizza-boy Tim and the motel room.

'Ah, mate, maybe twenty years ago I would have tried it on. I don't have the stamina now.'

I laughed, he laughed and we immediately bonded. I instantly felt safe. Dave oozed softness.

His truck was big and grand and he took a lot of pride in it. It turned out that many truckies did. He polished the steering wheel before we set off, and climbed on to the bonnet to clean the windscreen. Truckies have to have a certain amount of breaks within a certain amount of hours – they're all tracked and can be fined if they don't take enough time off the road. They get paid per kilometre so they all want to drive as many *kays* as they can a day, and they often find the enforced stopping time frustrating.

I offered to share my crisps with Dave as we waited.

'Nah, mate. I'm on a diet,' he responded as he tapped his belly, which protruded from his vest. 'You know those Chiko rolls?' Chiko rolls are found in every truck stop and service station in Australia. They're made of cabbage that's fried and then battered – a bit like a mix between a spring roll and a battered sausage, without the meat. They're very popular amongst truckies. 'Well, I used to have three a day,' he said. I can't imagine they're too good for someone who sits down to drive all day. I asked him when his last Chiko roll was, and when his diet had started? He blushed and looked embarrassed. 'Yesterday,' he replied, causing us both to laugh again.

When Dave wasn't working he cared for his wife. They'd been married for 20 years and for 12 of those years Dave had acted as her carer. One day, when they were getting ready to go out for the day, his wife slipped down the stairs and has had problems walking since. He'd taken more hours to drive trucks recently, as they needed the money. Driving trucks is a tough job. They're on the road driving thousands of kilometres day after day. Then he returned home and continued to work. I admired him a lot. I peeled an orange and offered him a segment. 'Nah, mate. That's too healthy.' I didn't know how long Dave was going to be on a diet for but I wished him luck.

Dave was staying the night in Meekatharra. I was broke and wanted to keep going to save money on accommodation, and it was only 8 p.m. Trucks drive through the night too so I thought I'd give it a go to find a lift. If I couldn't then I'd meet up with Dave in the morning. I saw a guy on the side of the road, lying beside his wheel, looking underneath his truck. He stepped up from the ground and wiped his hands on his shirt. I asked him if he was driving south that night.

He looked at Trevor then at me. Then he took a step back, folded his arms, looked at Trevor again and said, 'Were you walking up here a few months ago?'

I found out that Noel 'Black Chief' Power had his own truck company. He was almost 70 and should really have been retired, but he loved driving so much he was still at it. On the top of his windscreen was his name in two-foot letters. Again, he took a lot of pride in his truck, but he was having a few mechanical issues.

'Mate, if I get this lady going I'd love to give you a lift. I want to hear what you've been doing since I saw you walking back then.'

I sat inside the truck stop and read a book as I waited for the verdict.

Two hours later Noel threw the door open. 'Right, mate, hop in. We're off.'

I drifted in and out of sleep during the course of the night. I tried to fight it as I didn't want to appear rude as Noel had so kindly given me a lift. He chucked his *doona* (Australian for duvet) on me as he saw my head clanging on the window, suggesting that I was tired. 'Mate, don't worry,' he said, giving me the OK to nod off. These guys are machines with staying up through the night. Noel had only started his shift on leaving Meekatharra, so it was really his morning.

I woke to the orange sun blaring directly through the windscreen as it rose over the flat horizon. The views these guys see are incredible. They have some of the best offices in the world.

'Right, mate. I'm not going to Perth, so I'll see if I can get you a lift.'

I was still wiping the drool from the corner of my mouth and picking out the sleep in my eyes as I worked out what Noel meant. He pulled down the two-way radio that sat above the windscreen, and called out to truckies in the radius it covered.

'Noel Black Chief here. I've got a Pommie chick with me who's trying to get to Perth. Can anyone take her that way?'

The radio crackled as he waited for a response. A guy in front of us replied to say he worked for a big company and wasn't allowed. Another guy behind said the same.

We pulled into a service station in a town called Cue. I was still bleary-eyed and stumbled out of the door, which was six foot above the ground, as I tried to get my brain into gear to follow Noel. He bowled through the service-station doors, greeting the ladies behind the counter. They greeted him, calling him by his nickname. He handed me a tray of two coffees and two egg-and-bacon rolls and told me to sit down.

'Eat your breakfast. I'll be back in a sec.' I didn't even have time to offer him money.

A few minutes later, Noel emerged through the service-station doors again, flexing his biceps and announcing that he had found me a lift. Whilst I was eating the breakfast that he bought for me, he had scouted round the truck park asking the drivers if anyone was heading in my direction.

'Linds, this is Fingers. He's your next lift. Have a good one, mate,' Noel said as he wrapped his arms around me and patted me on the back. 'Look after her, mate,' he said to Fingers.

Fingers was an 'oversized escort' driver. He was also oversized himself, towering over me at six foot five. He drove a van to escort trucks that were carrying large stuff, which can take up the entire width of the highway. Any vehicle heading towards one would have a fright if it wasn't for people like Fingers who'd drive ahead with a flashing light and a sign on top of their van saying, *OVERSIZED VEHICLE*. He was on the road a lot too, so he'd got his own set-up in the back of his van. He packed away his coffee and put his things back in a drawer, which shut next to his bed. I hopped in and gave Noel one last wave as we drove away.

On one occasion when Fingers had been driving, the car in front of him suddenly stopped. Fingers slammed his foot on the brake, threw his hand up to the roof of his van for support and crashed into the back of the car ahead. He was fine, considering, but his hand was not. Some tools hadn't been packed away properly in the back of his van and these flew to the front, slicing three of his fingers entirely off. 'That's why I'm called Fingers,' he said.

Thousands of people from across the world descend on Western Australia from August to September to see the wild flowers. I had been a couple of weeks ahead of their blooming during my walk, only seeing the start of them slightly peeking out of the arid soil, but now the side of the highway was spoiled with wild flowers of every colour. We drove past scenes that would have had Jackson Pollock twitching for his paintbrush, the colours were so vivid. I ooohed and ahhed as if fireworks were exploding ahead of the windscreen.

'Sorry,' I said to Fingers, apologising for my squealing.

'Not at all, mate,' he replied. 'I drive this route every week. I take it for granted. You're reminding me to see the beauty in it again.' Fingers slowed down and peered to my side of the road. I looked at him to ask if everything was OK. 'Yeh, mate, I just saw a dead kangaroo.' Fingers told me that whenever he wasn't escorting a truck he'd always pull over if he saw a dead kangaroo. He'd check their pouch and if there was a joey, he'd take it home to rear. He'd had to stop recently because he now had ten pet kangaroos, and his wife and their dog weren't too happy about it.

Fingers dropped me off at a train stop in Perth. He enveloped me in his mammoth frame and thanked me for being his companion. I waved him off and waited for my friend to pick me up. A smile grew across my face as I thought about the softness of these big, burly truckie characters, their community and all the tales they'd told me. By the time my friend arrived, I'd already decided on my next adventure: Truck Tales – circumnavigating Australia solely by hitch-hiking with truck drivers. Which is what I did.

ABOUT LINDSEY

Lindsey has cycled the length of Africa, completed two Ironman triathlons, marathon-trained with Kenyans, roller-skated to Bude in a nude suit (because it rhymed) and run to Manchester with a ukulele she was going to busk with, which inadvertently led to her playing and singing on her local BBC radio station every other night. When her dad died, she sought solace in a book she had read while backpacking in Australia a few months beforehand. The book's characters would not only inspire her to deal with her grief but would lead her to a whole world of adventure.

Find out more about Lindsey at:

W: lindseycole.co.uk ♦ T: @LindseyCole
I: @stompycole ♦ F: @walkingtherabbitprooffence

22
GO AND WAKE UP YOUR LUCK

Lois Pryce enters Iran with
her 'forbidden' motorcycle,
a form of transport that is
outlawed for Iranian women...

Lois Pryce

It was a challenge to choose an extract for this collection – I knew it had to be from my travels in Iran but I was simply overwhelmed with options! The warmth and generosity of the Iranians was unlike anything I had experienced elsewhere in the world. It was not just the offers of food, tea and accommodation that appeared from nowhere each time I stopped, but the generosity of people's time, thought and conversation – their enthusiasm for human engagement. I could have chosen any number of stories – the truckers who ran me off the road in order to stuff my panniers with pomegranates, or the battle-scarred ex-army general who put his life on hold to show me his city, or the car full of shadowy figures that trailed me on a dark mountain road, only because they wanted to invite me to party with them. Eventually I chose this story from the very beginning of my journey. I chose it because it encapsulates the indefatigable spirit and humour of the Iranian people – and it was the moment I realised that by coming to Iran, alone on my motorcycle, something very special was about to unfold.

————

Riding my motorcycle east across Turkey, I was following the classic hippie trail of the sixties and seventies – but in the twenty-first century this route was a whole different story. Only a few decades ago the standard itinerary of Turkey–

Iran–Afghanistan–Pakistan had been the mind-opening rite of passage for thousands of wide-eyed British teens making their way to India. But now, a generation later, Iran stood isolated from the world; Kabul, once the swinging city of the Middle East, was reeling from war; the Buddhas of Bamiyan were blown to smithereens; and Pakistan had become a no-go zone, only accessible with military escorts for the few overland travellers prepared to run the gauntlet.

I was born too late for that innocent era; my world travels had coincided almost exactly with the so-called War on Terror. In the spring of 2003 I had left the safe but tedious confines of my BBC office job to ride my motorcycle from Alaska to Argentina, just as George Bush invaded Iraq. The Stars and Stripes were flying high on the first leg of that trip. But as soon as I crossed the border into Mexico it was a different story. And by the time I reached Central America the graffiti was already appearing – *BUSH GENOSIDA, ENEMIGO DE LA HUMANIDAD*. I spent a lot of time explaining that I was a UK passport holder, '*Soy Inglésa!*', not a war-mongering gringo from north of the border, and it seemed to help. But a few years later, while travelling through Muslim North Africa, that distinction had blurred: our 'special relationship' meant that as far as the rest of the world was concerned, we were all in it together. Border guards saw my passport and spat Tony Blair's name into the sandy ground as they issued a grudging entry stamp. '*Hey! I was on that anti-war march in 2003*,' I wanted to tell them. But what good would it do? As much good as the march itself. In the intervening years London had been shaken by the 7/7 bombings, and in 2007, when I emerged from the Algerian Sahara to discover that Saddam Hussein had been killed, I knew that the days of chatting with immigration officials about David Beckham and Princess Diana were over. Now, taking my first foray into the Middle East, to a country famous for its hostility towards Britain, I felt a mixture of sadness, anger, regret and shame, albeit for actions for which I wasn't personally responsible but which still hung heavy on my shoulders. The great British passport had lost its lustre, and its pompous statement on the inside cover – 'Her Britannic Majesty's Secretary of State requests and requires in the Name of Her Majesty all those whom it may concern to allow the bearer to pass freely without let or hindrance, and to afford the bearer such assistance and protection as may be necessary' – seemed vaguely ridiculous. Good luck with that, Ma'am.

My first taste of the East had appeared in the shape of Istanbul, with its thrilling skyline of minarets and domes and the mighty Bosphorus Bridge shuttling traffic between Europe and Asia. But as I continued eastwards my confidence began to wane. Although I had been issued a visa to enter Iran and to travel independently, it was on the condition that I use public transport while in the country. The Iranian Ministry of Foreign Affairs had essentially forbidden me to travel around by motorcycle. This ruling had messed with my master plan so I had taken the 'executive' decision to ignore it and had set off on my bike nonetheless. My loose plan was to head for the Turkish–Iranian border and somehow sneak my motorcycle across the frontier. Quite how I was going to do this was still up for grabs.

The further I got from home, the twitchier I became. The long days in the saddle, across Turkey's lonely Pontic mountains, allowed my imagination to concoct all sorts of dramatic stories which involved me being turned away at the border, arrested for spying, escaping from my cell and hitching a ride in a truck full of contraband booze, and making a midnight crossing via some obscure smugglers' route in the mountains. The Iranian authorities' mistrust was contagious: they were paranoid about me, and now I was paranoid about them.

My arrival in Ankara, the functional, if rather dreary, capital of Turkey, stilled my fevered imagination and offered an agreeable, if less theatrical, answer to my problem – the Trans-Asia Express, a weekly rail service between there and Tehran. Its first Iranian destination was Tabriz, the north-western city just over the frontier that I had planned as my first stop. For the price of a few kebabs I could put myself and my bike on the train across the rest of Turkey and be deposited just inside Iran, 1,000 miles away. Hopefully once there, I could slip the bike out of the guard's van and be on my way, no questions asked. I felt quietly confident; my bike's paperwork was all in order and I was relying on bureaucratic incompetence: that the 'no-motorcycle' missive had failed to filter down to the immigration guards on the ground.

Much to the bemusement of Ankara's commuters, I pushed my bike through the busy station, over a level crossing and on to platform two, where it was heaved into the goods wagon by a gang of surly Turkish railway workers in greasy shirts. At the shriek of the guard's whistle, everyone climbed aboard and I found myself alone in a four-berth sleeping carriage. There was a time when my younger motorcycling self, who valued the notion of purism, would have been aggrieved by interrupting the ride like this, but purism be damned! Outwitting the Iranian authorities was my priority, and besides, as a secret railway fan, I was geekily excited about the idea of riding such a romantically titled train.

After an unhurried, two-day journey we arrived the following evening at Lake Van, in the mountainous wilderness of eastern Turkey. Here the baggage car was uncoupled from the train, trundled on to a ferry with a section of railway tracks embedded in its hold, and I and the other few hundred passengers climbed aboard the ferry for a five-hour sailing across the lake. On the eastern shore the baggage car would be hauled out of the ferry and hooked up to an Iranian train, which we would all board and continue on our way. It seemed a strangely convoluted way of getting to the other side of a lake. Why didn't they just continue the tracks around its edge? I couldn't understand it, but when I asked my fellow passengers the reason, nobody knew. They shrugged their shoulders, laughed and seemed unconcerned. I wondered, not for the first time when finding myself confronted with foreign illogicality, if my obsession with efficiency was a character trait peculiar to northern Europe. I decided I needed to lighten up – what the heck if they want to waste loads of time and effort hauling trains on to boats? It made for an interesting diversion and meant I got to hang out with more of my Iranian travelling companions, most of whom seemed to be entertaining themselves by taking photos of each other shinning up a giant flagpole on the deck and clambering up and down rickety service ladders. I watched them swinging off the top, whooping and laughing with apparently no concern for their safety; it was exhilarating to see and particularly refreshing that nobody tried to stop them. I stood on the deck, alone in the darkening evening, cheered by the clowning going on all around me. It made me feel at home; this was the kind of thing my friends and I would get up to. But I was surprised. My image of Iran was not that of a nation out for a laugh and a good time; I had expected Iranians to take a more solemn approach to life. My preconceptions were already unravelling fast.

On the eastern side of the lake the Iranian train was nowhere to be seen but nobody grumbled. In fact, it barely warranted a mention. So we all squeezed into a waiting room, furnished with nothing but a few plastic chairs, and did what the room was designed for.

Eventually, an Iranian railway official, dressed casually in an open-necked shirt, began herding us into some sort of line in order to allocate us carriages and seats. Next to me in the melee that passed for a queue was an elderly Iranian woman, dressed in the head-to-toe black chador, tightly wrapped around her neck and hairline with only the oval of her face visible, wrinkled and weathered from decades of Middle Eastern sun. She kept staring at me, her features large and expressive, although I was having trouble working out exactly what it was she was trying to express. Many of the other women were dressed in Western outfits and some had their hair exposed as we were still officially on Turkish soil, but this woman's clothing suggested a devout Islamic faith and all the traditional values that accompany it. I felt nervous under her gaze, sensing her criticism. This was the Iran I had feared, disapproval from a nation of hard-line Islamists, angered by the nerve of my infidel jaunt around their country. I shifted awkwardly, reluctant to lose my place in the 'queue' but fearing the situation that I sensed was brewing.

She came at me with a jabbing knotty finger. 'You, you have motor, yes?'

I must have appeared confused because she repeated it again but this time she accompanied it with the universal motion for twisting the throttle, complete with engine revving noises.

'Vroom, vroom! You have motor, yes? It is you?'

There was no point in denying it. Almost everyone in this room had seen my bike being loaded on to the train in Ankara, and anyone who had missed the spectacle had heard about it by now, via the Trans-Asia telegraph. There is no anonymity for the lone female British biker in Iran. I had a sudden cold fear that she was a spy for the Iranian Ministry of Foreign Affairs. Had she got wind of my bike-smuggling plan? Maybe I was on some kind of 'no vehicle' list after all. I got a grip on my fevered imagination and fessed up.

'Er, yes, that's me. I have motor, yes.'

I awaited a steely grip on my wrist but instead she grabbed hold of my face with her strong fleshy hands. Then she landed an enthusiastic smack on my cheek as a huge smile erupted across her stern features.

'Very good! Very good!' she bellowed at eardrum-piercing volume, hugging me into the voluminous folds of her chador.

Now she was jumping up and down, whacking me on the back and squeezing my face again, hooting with laughter. 'Very good! Very good! Vroom, vroom!'

Her motorcycle actions became more animated until she was imitating the moves of a daredevil speedway racer, body swerving from side to side, hips swinging beneath yards of billowing black fabric. She spoke excitedly in Persian to her friend, who translated for her.

'She says she wishes you every blessing for your journey.'

The old lady took my face in her hands again and stared into my eyes with such feeling I was almost compelled to look away. She said something I couldn't understand and then smiled, repeating it, gripping my face even harder, eyes still fixed on mine.

I looked to her friend for a translation. She nodded and smiled too.

'It is a saying we have in Iran,' she said. 'It means: go and wake up your luck.'

ABOUT LOIS

Lois Pryce is a British travel writer and author of three books about her motorcycle travels in the Americas, Africa and Iran. She has written for *The Telegraph*, *The Guardian*, *The New York Times*, CNN and *The Independent*, and was named by *The Telegraph* as one of the Ten Great Female Travellers. With her husband, adventure film-maker Austin Vince, she is co-founder/director of the Adventure Travel Film Festival, which occurs annually in the UK and Australia.

Find out more about Lois at:

W: www.loisontheloose.com
T: @LoisPryce ◆ F: Lois Pryce

23
KINDNESS TASTES LIKE A PIRANHA

Teachers pop up in unexpected places. For Pip Stewart, a life lesson came in the form of a small girl wielding a machete and a piranha...

Pip Stewart

know my cooking skills aren't great, but I wasn't expecting to be shown up in the middle of Brazil's Amazon. Least of all by a six-year-old girl wielding a machete and a piranha. She grinned and handed it to me – expertly descaled. Did I mention that this had all been done while she balanced on a slippery log that was protruding over the lake where we were working? The knife skills of an assassin, the agility of a gymnast; this girl kicked ass. I wasn't going to attempt to copy the manoeuvre for fear of ending up wet and, knowing my luck, blood-drenched. I clearly need to practise more tree poses in yoga armed with a sharp blade.

She gestured with the machete that this particular toothy piranha specimen was to join the numerous others flapping in a pewter bowl on the shoreline. I let out a squeal as the fish writhed around in my hands. If a piranha had a death rattle this was likely it. I prayed it didn't have jaw-locking reflexes too...

The girl looked at me with amusement at my skittishness. Or maybe it was my inability to descale a fish as quickly as the children. In a quick life audit I realised that if this was a survival situation I was absolutely certain that my life would be entirely at the mercy of a small, lithe, machete-carrying, Amazonian child from the Mundurukú indigenous community. Bugger.

My life motto is that everyone can teach you something, and in the arse end of the jungle I was surrounded by teachers. I was spending time with the community as part of a documentary looking into how deforestation is impacting the indigenous people that call the Amazon home. We've lost around 20 per cent of the rainforest already due to pressures such as illegal logging, gold-mining and monoculture farming – crops like palm oil, soya beans and cocoa. Then there's the dam building. In 2016, the Mundurukú community managed to halt plans for the controversial São Luiz do Tapajós dam hydroelectric project. A project which would flood their homelands, damage their fish stocks and, ultimately, their way of life. Although stopped for now, they are fearful that the project could be resurrected.

I'd been invited by one of the chiefs of the community, Valdemar Saw Mundurukú, to witness an ancient fishing ceremony that takes place once a year. The ceremony, known as *tinguejada*, involved the entire community moving from the village, travelling upriver to the deep jungle. After a hike through the forest, dragging dugout canoes, camping gear and pretty much an entire village with us, we hit upon a lake that had been cut off from the main part of the river due to the summer's low water levels.

I was fascinated; within about 30 minutes, hammocks, fires and tarpaulin shelters had sprung up in the jungle – men, women and children all playing a part. Pet monkeys too were brought up for the event, swinging in the hammocks with the kids who were bestowing them with cuddles and kisses galore. I was witnessing the construction of a jungle city. Left to my own devices I doubt I would have lasted the night in the jungle. This was made painfully clear when it was pointed out to me that I was trying to tie my hammock under a wasp's nest. It turns out common sense is a useful life skill wherever you are. Watching the community interact so seamlessly with nature highlighted how isolated my life in London is from what is ultimately the most natural way of living – and how much I was depending on them for guidance.

The ritual was the most fascinating thing that I have ever witnessed. Before the fishing starts, what can only be described as an elaborate form of kiss chase ensues. Members of the opposite sex chase each other and cover their target in sticky, white, gloopy tree resin. Cue screaming, running through the jungle (made to look easy barefoot or in flip-flops) and laughter galore. Apparently, every member of the community needs to be coated in the stuff for the fishing to be a success. Although new to this, I do have one tip if you ever find yourself in such a situation: avoid the eyes. Thick, clumpy gunk in the eye does not aid fishing – or vision, for that matter. I speak from experience.

Rather awkwardly, the chief explained that women on their period and pregnant women are not meant to bathe in the river to wash off the resin. Something to do with turning the cheek of the fish red or some such. Admittedly, I didn't hear a great deal through my now-clogged ears so the explanation may have been entirely different. I faced a dilemma. I was covered head to toe in white sticky resin which, incidentally, was forming attractive, solid lumps in my eyelashes, hair and eyebrows. I desperately needed a wash. At the same time I didn't fancy the wrath of the Mundukurús should my menstruation upset centuries of tradition and ritual. Yes, on balance, a lack of a dip seemed the best course of action.

I based myself in the nearest wooden dugout canoe and grabbed my shower – a bucket – and desperately began trying to get the clumps of sticky resin out from my hair. Imagine, if you will, less a wet T-shirt competition and more a fully clothed, pale swamp monster spluttering and gurgling away under torrents of brown murky water. Clearly I was a newbie with tree resins as within a few minutes I had several ladies and children applying oil and soap to my hair, trying to help me comb it out. Sitting in the base of what was now a waterlogged canoe, in wet pants and a soggy, white-stained, adhesive shirt, I couldn't have felt more cared for than if I'd been in a swanky London beauty salon. Apparently this was far more entertaining than the average hair wash too as we drew quite a crowd. Although I think this might have had something to do with the deep guffawing that emanated from all of us involved.

As dusk approached, the men of the community moved to a small clearing and started bashing up a poisonous tree root known as *timbó*. A tree root so deadly it's often used for committing suicide, according to the community. Once the root was suitably smashed, exposing some of the fatal sap, the elders put it away until the morning. Campfires were lit, hot drinks produced, and occasional flashlights poked their way through the dark night, checking on the now-sleeping children.

'Sleep,' I was told. 'We will wake you.' I lay in my hammock, looking through the holes in the mosquito net, watching the distinctive shape of bottoms in hammocks swaying away and fires in the distance flickering. The jungle roars to life at night but it's unbelievably peaceful. Magical, in fact. I was flooded with an incredible feeling of love. Here, in the forest full of things that Google tells me can kill me, I felt incredibly safe and happy. Language barriers mattered not one bit: actions truly speak louder than words.

I know this was a special place because my love for humanity held despite a 3-a.m. wake-up call. Get in the way of my sleep or food and we usually have a problem on our hands. Today, however, I was more intrigued than grumpy. I threw on a hoodie to stem the morning chill and headed down to the lake. The men of the community prepared their fishing nets and their dugout canoes before slipping off over the shining black lake. Mist was rising over the water, which gave an eerie glow to the proceedings. Occasional flashes of torchlight would be seen skimming over the water. As the men lowered down the sap, the fish became paralysed and stunned by the stupefying root.

On the shoreline, I was sitting with the other women, who were relighting the fires and boiling water, and the children who were beginning to stir. Valdemar had stayed behind too and began to tell me, through the help of my fixer, that their way of life was becoming massively threatened by outside interests. This fishing ritual only happens once a year, respecting the land and giving the fish time to breed, yet corporate dangers could wipe out their traditions completely.

'This jungle will exist for many generations because we are not letting people come to take the wood or the fruits. This is why we fight to keep our land and our forest – the forest that sustains the fish, the game, the meat, the fruits that we eat. This is why we don't want to see a dam. We want to see the beautiful rocks in the middle of the river, the islands, the birds, the river dolphins. If they dam the river everything will disappear.'

As the sun began to rise so did more and more dying fish. Boys, too young to go out on the boats, were darting around the shoreline with their spears trying to pluck the fish out of the water. The rest of us worked to descale, salt and then cook the haul. After hours of work I was presented with a plastic plate.

My fish came with a warning: you may get the shits. Apparently if you've never come into contact with the sap before it can be rather disruptive on the old digestive system.

Despite the prophecy of things to come, as I tucked into my now-salted toothy friend I couldn't help but feel that this was the best fish I'd ever eaten. This fish had brought us together. It represented a community struggling to protect its way of life from outside interests. It represented both opportunity and danger: what can be achieved when we work together or against each other.

It's often the smallest gestures that make the biggest impact in life. For me, kindness came in the form of a piranha. Crouching on that wet log with a smiling six-year-old, both of us covered in newly flaked fish scales, tree resin and mosquito bites, I'd never felt more part of a community – even if my contribution was limited to court jester. Age, place of birth, machete-wielding ability – it didn't matter. We worked as one with nature. We were all needed. We were all accepted. United by sticky tree resin and a common purpose, we were no longer individuals: we were a team out there in the jungle – a metaphor, perhaps, for how we should live. Something struck me as I gingerly held the fish in my hand. The ultimate kindness of all: I was no longer a stranger. I never was.

ABOUT PIP

Pip Stewart is a journalist and adventurer who has reported all over the world for the likes of CNN, the BBC, Red Bull, *The Telegraph* and the *South China Morning Post*. A self-proclaimed hippy at heart, Pip is a firm believer that connecting with people and the great outdoors is good for the soul. Her mantra in life is that everyone can teach you something.

Pip is no stranger to sweating for a story – she's cycled halfway around the world (Malaysia to London), and travelled across the remote Amazon basin by bike, boat and terrifyingly small planes, for a six-part documentary highlighting the impact that deforestation is having on indigenous communities. In April 2018 she returned from the Amazon jungle once again, having completed a world first paddle – a source to sea descent of Guyana's Essequibo river.

Pip has a master's in journalism from the University of Hong Kong and a bachelor's in Modern History and Politics from Oxford University. She's currently based in London – usually plotting an escape.

––––––

Find out more about Pip at:

W: www.PhillippaStewart.com ✦ T: @Stewart_Pip
I: @pipstewart ✦ F: @PipStewartAdventure

24

A NUBIAN TALE

After spending eight months cycling through Europe and the Middle East, Rebecca thought she had mastered the art of bike touring. But when she ran out of water in the Sahara, she realised how much she still had to learn – and how deeply reliant she was on the support and care of others

Rebecca Lowe

I know things have taken a turn for the worse when my mother turns up unexpectedly in the desert. It's often a worrying sign when one's mother turns up unexpectedly anywhere, but right here, right now, it seems a particular cause for concern.

What 'here' means is somewhat unclear for a start. I'm certainly far enough from anywhere to feel afraid, and close enough to feel a fool: two states of mind that have become troublingly familiar of late. If pushed on the subject, 'now' is admittedly murky too. Is it afternoon or evening? Dinner time or dusk? How long have I been here, under this blinding, yellow-white sky?

On the roadside, I lie beside a curdled sea. To my right and left, vast sand sheets stretch to the horizon, where most living things have long burned away. The conditions are extreme, and in the weeks I have been here I feel I have burned away too, turning slowly to ash as I've urged myself on.

Now, eyes half-closed, I breathe in... *one, two...* then out. Under my head is a pannier, dusty and stiff, detached from the broken rear rack of my bicycle. I lie like a starfish, fingers splayed, legs and arms spread wide. I know I mustn't stay here, but I feel transfixed. Everything is heavy now, and the ground is soft as silk.

Soon I sense I am drifting and the world is fading. In the distance, my mother's shaky outline seems to swim against the sun. 'Just a trick of the light,' I murmur. 'Get up and pull yourself together.' But all I do is descend, as if tugged lightly, persistently, from below.

I think about today and yesterday, and how I came to be lying out here now, alone. Half-formed thoughts in my half-conscious state. It began, as these things often do, with a change of plan. And a bearded man with a stick. 'Old Dongola,' he said, pointing across the Nile while thumbing a thin, greying pamphlet. He showed me pictures of old granite columns, some upright, some fallen, and a rhomboid fortress on a hill. 'Yes,' I replied. 'Great.' And so it came to be.

Old Dongola. It had a ring to it, a hint of Cuban sea dog or Venetian gondolier. I imagined lush fields and waterfalls; hot springs and saturnalia; holy grails and unicorns. Google Maps showed 200 kilometres of nothing, admittedly, but what kind of modern Atlantis wouldn't shield itself from the hordes?

The journey took half a day. There was a tangle of palms, mango groves and *al-harra* trees, jungle-thick. A blue boat. A pink house. And burning, soupy sands, where my bike sank like a stone.

There were blundering chickens and *jalabiya*-robed men. And a grey metal shack, where topless policemen watched manatees mating on TV. 'Next year I move to Riyadh,' a young officer told me. 'There you have the money; here you have the life.'

'Money first, then life?' I suggested. He stared at me, flexing his guns. 'You look like Mesut Özil in those glasses,' he said.

I arrived shortly before sundown. Trekking out to the ruins, I passed domed mud-brick tombs, crumbling walls and the rotting carcass of a hyena. I found the rhomboid fortress, proud but forlorn, and climbed high into the battlements. At the top, I felt like a fallen queen. Fourteen hundred years ago I'd have been staring at a kingdom, the capital of Nubia: first Christian, later Muslim. Now lost to all.

Down below was the Nile, and on its banks a sharp slash of green and brown where the desert choked the foliage as if snuffing out a candle. And I found myself thinking about these snuffed-out people, these Nubians, buried by history and the ever-shifting lines in the sand.

As darkness fell, I made my way back to the road. I found a man with a Toyota truck, busted and rough-hewn, who took me to a house several hours from the tarmac track. Here I was served *ful* and yogurt, and kindly given a bed, while droves of children sat by my nose and worked in shifts to watch me sleep.

I awoke to a morning full of light and date palms and a dry sweetness to the air. And a new road leading south, half sunk beneath the dunes.

At first I enjoyed the ride. A few trucks passed, dusting me in a crisp film of grit, but mainly I was alone. I felt strong, and more free and calm than I had been for months. For over half a year I'd been on my bike, slogging across hot asphalt, cool grasslands, loose dirt. But the Sahara was something new; there was a power there, but a purity too. It was dazzling and shattering, and each day it bled me dry.

Water was always a struggle. I bought bottles from shacks and topped up from roadside urns, filled by locals for passers-by. I drank constantly, though it never seemed enough. Today my supplies dwindled quickly. The sun was brutal, hotter than before. Sweat streamed down my face, chest and back, forming pools around my waist.

An hour went by, then two, and soon my water was gone. But there were no shacks on this road, and all but the first of the urns had been dry.

As the sun rose higher, I slowed to a crawl. To my left was endless nothing, and overhead a shining sky. Far to my right, the curves of the Nile glinted and teased: an artery through cracked skin. Head bowed, I kept my sights on the horizon; it steadied me somehow, though I knew I'd never reach it. *Plod on,* I thought on loop, channelling Ranulph Fiennes as I always do in these moments. *Plod on. Plod on. Plod forever.*

The wind was rough and coarse-grained. It whipped up dust skeletons that skittered across my path, spinning in a jerky dance. They grazed my eyes and lips, and dragged tears across my cheeks. One pulled me off the road, where I bumped over rocks and thorns before forcing my way back on. *Plod on,* I kept thinking. *Plod on. Plod on. Plod forever.*

Around me, everything seemed immense. I felt crushed by the Sahara's beauty and the crassness of its strength. I felt overwhelmed.

I felt tired.

It wasn't long before I stopped. I don't recall the exact moment I did, just a series of instants blinking like stop-motion film. What I remember clearly is the urn: a single clay pot a few hundred metres from the road, shaded under bamboo. I remember weighing my options: leave my bicycle and walk out, as the sun dipped low, or press on to arrive somewhere – anywhere – before dark. The first option didn't appeal. My lights had been stolen in Egypt and the blackness of the desert was complete. In just over an hour I'd be blind.

But I needed water more than I needed light – even dirty water, squeezed in tiny droplets through a filter. Even if there was only a faint chance of success, and it risked killing my dazed momentum and made it hard to go on. So I pulled over and dismounted, and laid my bike on the ground. And I remember the feeling as I left the road, the faint nausea of muted panic. I remember the final steps, and steadying my hands on the rim. I remember that I knew before I looked, and that suddenly it seemed inevitable. That, of course, there was no water.

I recall being back on the road, staring into space. I believe I stood there for a long time, slowly shutting down. The tiredness crept inside like a cancer, spreading from limb to limb and bringing me to my knees. And then I heaved; three, four, five dry heaves, bent double, ejecting specks of acrid phlegm. *Come on*, I thought. *Plod ON.*

And then: *Damn you, Fiennes. I can't.*

When I lay down I'm not sure. But it felt good. The ground opened beneath me, enveloping my sore back and legs. Here was my feather bed, my lotus field, and for just a moment I closed my eyes.

For just a moment.

I sense I am drifting and the world is fading. Get up, I am thinking...

Get up get up get up get up get up get up get up get up get up get up get up get up...

GET UP, YOU STOOOOOPID GIRL!!

I jerk awake with a start. And yet still the voice booms large: familiar, imperative, with a hint of heyday Zsa Zsa Gabor.

DAAAAHling! Didn't I tell you not to be so foooolish as to die in the desert all alone?

I sit up and gasp like a swimmer surfacing, taking mad, hot gulps of air. Scanning the landscape, I search for the small, feverish Hungarian with a powerful bosom and purposeful stomp. But all I see is sand and sky, forever. As quickly as she arrived, she's gone, along with the djinns and dust devils drawing me to the ground.

A Nubian Tale   **Rebecca Lowe**

I climb to my feet, feeling both leaden and feather-light. *Only you, Mother,* I think. *Only your nagging could invade my dreams halfway across the world.* But I know that now, as ever, she's right to be peeved.

My thermometer reached the mid-forties today, although it admittedly hasn't been entirely trustworthy since falling in the toilet in Egypt. It could be cooler. Or hotter. All I know is how I feel, and the signs aren't good. My tongue is bloated, my throat a thousand tiny knives. My temple throbs, and feels curiously taut about my skull.

I heave up Maud, my bike, who lies at my feet. After 6,000 miles together, from London to the depths of Sudan, it doesn't feel so lonely knowing she's out here with me. Yet she has no brain or flesh to feed, and struggles to empathise at moments like these. She also has no means of movement other than my own shrivelled-husk legs, which I can't help but hold against her right now.

For the first time on the trip, I feel worried. It's one thing expiring out here all alone, after all; it's another doing so in express defiance of my mother. I find myself thinking back to the Sunday lunch when I first told her of my plan to cycle alone through the Middle East. She took it well, considering. At least, she didn't burn my passport or call the local sanatorium to have me committed. She did send me an email later, however, to clarify her feelings in case there had been any ambiguity. 'You cannot imagine how devastated I feel...' it began, before launching into a calm and measured analysis of the potential pitfalls I should prepare for along the way. The words 'dangerous', 'awful', 'reckless', 'hostile', 'juvenile', 'arrest', 'dangerous' (again), 'terrible worry', 'risking life and limb', 'robbed and raped' and 'family disintegrating' were all used

261

to persuasive effect, alongside a restrained smattering of a dozen or so exclamation marks to emphasise the particularly salient points.

I had of course done what any loving daughter would do in such circumstances: hugged and kissed and comforted and reassured and continued doing exactly as I pleased without giving it any further thought. But now, as I stand in quiet desperation under a darkening sky, a thought occurs to me – the unnerving thought every child is forced to confront at some point in their lives. *What if my mother was right?*

Holding Maud steady, I step astride her and take a few long breaths. Going on feels both inevitable and impossible. 'Plod forever,' I say aloud, willing myself. And then: 'Sorry for before, Ranulph. You know how it can be.'

Who can say how long I cycle for? Time passes in circles and drifts, as if in a dream. I ride with my head down, sheathed in sweat and shivering. I stray loosely across the road, as if skirting black ice. I sing quietly and recite poems – mainly 'Jabberwocky' and dirty versions of A. A. Milne verses – to hear myself, and to remember I exist.

For much of the journey I seem to hover outside myself, watching from afar – a coping mechanism I've come to know well. This other me is wry, detached, and finds the most agonising event absurd. *Look at you,* she says, dripping with scorn. *Eight months of cycling and still such an ass. No wonder you were thrown out of the Brownies as a girl.*

I think about my boyfriend, and my family and parents. When I last saw my father, he was lying drugged up in a hospital bed. He had been diagnosed with chronic lymphocytic leukaemia, and during the chemo had contracted a blood infection that spread to his heart and brain. He had maybe two months, the doctors told us – but Dad, it seems, disagreed. By the time I left his bedside, he was chatting up nurses and demanding beer. Nearly 90 years old and still the fighter he always was, rising from the ashes even as the condolence cards poured in.

Plod on. Plod on. Plod forever.

I think about my friends and how much they mean to me, and how saying this always feels trite. I think about my bed at home, and how long it is since I've lain in it. I think about the hundreds of people I've met on this trip, and the generosity I'll never repay.

After a time, I think of nothing but water. I see it all around me, hovering like a Tartarus punishment out of reach. I watch it shimmering in the distance, in pools of curved light. I feel its silken touch on my tongue, and crashing in foamy crescents over my head.

Thirst is a crazy thing. It postures and raves, breathing fire. I struggle to contain it, and at one point pull over to help steel my nerves. On the back of a postcard I scrawl spidery notes in a rush: *Hallucnating* [sic]. *Confused. Terrified.*

As I ride, I watch as the sun turns electric pink and bleeds through creases in the sky. The sight of it thrills me, and I urge myself on harder. Beside me, twilight shapes twirl and melt, and some I swear are laughing.

When the light goes, I am nearly gone too. My face is hot and dry, my hands strangely chilled. I see the distant glow of a town and turn towards it like a turtle hatchling drawn to the sea. On my way in, I skid on a sand drift and I'm too tired to prevent the fall.

I don't know who finds me. But I recall lying for a while with a mouth full of dust; and being held upright while water is poured down my throat; and vomiting it up, mortified and mumbling apologies. And not long afterwards being placed on a donkey cart that jolts and rocks as it takes me off the road.

At a drinks stall, I am given more water – four, six, eight bottles – and gulp it too quickly, willing it down. Nausea rises in waves, and my eyes cannot focus. Yet I feel my body moisten and unfurl, even as I turn to heave.

Later, a group of men lead me to a house and into a darkened room. Inside is a wooden wardrobe and three *angareebs* (string beds) beneath a slow ceiling fan that squeaks with each rotation. The air is thick with heat. Several women enter and leave, bringing bedding, water and juice. Then I am left alone.

For a long time I lie there, dozing in fevered fits and starts. Then, without knowing, I fall into a deep and dreamless sleep.

At 5 a.m., I awake with the dawn. It's a morning I'll always remember, because the thought hits me instantly, as clear and sweet as birdsong.

I'm OK.

Ribbons of light spill through the window and I breathe them in, savouring their warmth. I still feel weak, but the delirium has gone. The world is sharp and steady again, full of colour and crystal lines. *I'm OK*, I think. *I'm OK.* I drink two bottles of juice with rehydration salts, but pick tentatively at my food; my stomach remains delicate, and I'm reluctant to disgrace myself again.

When I get up, everyone is sleeping except an older woman, who leads me to a small mud bathroom that opens to the sky. I shower using a metal bucket, tipping the water over my head and shoulders and letting it pool about my feet. It is delicious and cool, and the feeling of it fills me with pure joy and astonishment. I know I wash for too long, too wastefully, but I can't get over the simple wonder of it – the wild beauty of this moment, under the water and under the sky.

Afterwards I see where I am. The building is an adobe bungalow, split into five rooms arranged around a central courtyard. In the kitchen there's a fridge, stove and cluster of metal pans, and in a bedroom an ancient TV and DVD player. Outside there's a water tank and a lone blue, plastic chair. This is all they have – the people who showed me such care and took me into their home.

Soon these people join me. They are Nubian, like most in this region, and they cluster around me as they wake. There are ten children – nine girls and one baby boy – who call me Becca and Paprika, and try on my helmet for size. Looking after them are five women, draped in vibrant cloth, who bring me milky tea and sugared toast, and urge their daughters to play outside.

I warm to them immediately. This isn't always the case; yesterday a group of bothersome children ruined my night by attacking me for hours with henna ('*Sooo beautiful,*' they cried deludedly, as my luminescent hands lit up the sky). But this family is patient and kind, and the young girls sweet. They are also politely curious, asking endless questions from a dog-eared English phrase book. 'You have husband?' a younger woman enquires. 'You… leave… husband?' She laughs, and the others clutch their sides chuckling.

The women take me on a tour of the village: a poor neighbourhood of crumbling walls, skinny goats and stray dogs slumped in mud-caked puddles. Few men are present, but two approach me when our group passes by. One seems about 14 and wears a *flydubai* shirt; the other is robed in a traditional *jalabiya* and is perhaps 60 years older, or more.

'Hello,' the younger one says. 'Bilal.'

'Rebecca.'

'Why?' He pauses, trying to find the right word. 'Why... come Sudan?'

I shrug, giving the answer I know will please the most. 'Sudan *hilwa*.' 'Beautiful' is always one of the first words I learn in a new country, after 'hello', 'how are you' and 'kebab'.

He smiles. 'Where now?'

'Karima.'

The older man glances up. His eyes are large and watery, and he has a missing front tooth. He says a few words in Arabic, nodding his head animatedly, and the boy translates.

'He asks: you will see pyramids? At Nuri? Very old. Nubian.'

'I very much want to, yes.'

'Good. He says you must see them, and tell others. Then come and see us again!'

I have heard of the pyramids, and their pride is not misplaced. The Nubians were one of the earliest settlers on the Nile, developing into an advanced and powerful civilisation. These tombs are testament to the dominion they once held, built for Nubian pharaohs who once stunned the world by conquering the mighty Egyptian lands to the north. The oldest date from the seventh century bce – yet over time their stories were lost.

'I will,' I assure them. 'Of course.'

'And you have tea now?'

I nod again – 'thank you' – and return his warm grin.

They bring me milky tea, then lead me to another door. Inside, an elderly lady sits in a dark room on a broken *angareeb*, surrounded by plastic bottles and debris. A black headscarf frames her plump, leathery face, bunched up around the neck of an embroidered tunic. After Bilal introduces me, she stands unsteadily, grips both my wrists and speaks in a whisper.

'She says: welcome! You are lucky for us,' Bilal tells me. 'God has brought you and will keep you safe.'

I thank her, feeling oddly reassured, and she looks at me fondly. 'And she says: you are welcome to stay here,' Bilal adds, with a smile. 'You must meet her son. Perhaps you marry him?'

The woman cackles, and grips my wrists harder. 'Very sadly I must move on,' I say, and Bilal's smile broadens. 'No problem – she will wait!'

Back at the house, I prepare Maud for the road. I'm not sure I'm ready to continue, but the heat has softened and I vow to take it slowly. I've now returned to the south side of the Nile, as it skims the top of the volcanic Bayuda Desert and folds back on itself towards Karima, and I know there are rest stops along the way. Today, hopefully, the elements won't throw me to the wolves.

As I pack, the women press bread and biscuits into my bags. They seem worried about me leaving, but I insist I feel fine. Their concern is touching, and in the courtyard I start to cry. I hug each of them in turn, and try to give them money but they forcefully refuse. Instead, I press my hand to my heart and repeat, 'Thank you, thank you, *shukran*', and give one of the girls a small wooden magnet shaped like a leaf. It feels like a pitiful token, but I hope they can see that to me it means much more.

As I leave, an older lady rushes up from the gate, clutching a stack of *kisra* flatbread and a bottle of water. She stuffs the bread into my hands, then tips the bottle to her mouth as if drinking. 'Water! Good!' she says, passing it to me and laughing, and everyone else laughs too. I thank her and take a few swigs, delighting in the taste and watching droplets glint silver on my sleeve.

I smile and give a thumbs up, and everyone laughs again. Then I start to pedal, carving a slender furrow through the sand.

ABOUT REBECCA

Rebecca is a freelance journalist from London who specialises in human rights and the Middle East. She spent a year cycling to Iran, via the Middle East and North Africa, in the hope of learning more about this deeply misunderstood region of the world and telling the stories of the people who live there. Her mother has finally forgiven her for the endeavour.

Find out more about Rebecca at:

W: www.thebicyclediaries.co.uk ♦ T: @reo_lowe

I: @bexio8 ♦ F: @bexbicyclediaries

25

THE ROAD FROM PETAUKE

It's not just fear that dwells in the heart of the night...

Rudi Stark

left Lusaka early despite an awful night's sleep. Determined to escape the chaos of peak morning traffic, I hurriedly packed the truck and sneaked out of the city. I had a good seven-hour journey ahead before reaching South Luangwa National Park. The park would be my last stopover before heading into Malawi and turning north once again, with London waiting somewhere far over the distant horizon.

My confidence was still somewhat shaken after nearly drowning my trusty old Land Cruiser in Botswana. I had resolved to avoid any further misadventures, knowing full well that the African continent would not let me off that easily. Coordinates entered into my GPS, favourite playlist updated, I left the waking city behind and was greeted by the sort of sunrise that brushes aside all doubt that a benevolent creator exists. Alone, with the familiar rattling of my old truck beneath me, wilderness stretching out on either side of the Great Eastern Road, the sky a painting Turner himself would have envied, I was filled with euphoria.

The miles drifted by at a contented pace, the mammoth potholes keeping me honest, and soon my GPS was instructing me to turn from the main road as I entered the small town of Petauke. It was three in the afternoon as I pulled over to stretch my legs and fill up with fuel. The fuel stop was little more than a single pump on a crumbling concrete slab beneath a small, rotting wooden roof, a convenience store with half-empty shelves to one side. Nobody there spoke any English – very few do in the rural parts of Zambia – but with enthusiastic hand gestures and exaggerated facial expressions, I managed to get the old truck filled. Eighty-odd miles remained to Mfuwe – the gateway to Luangwa – and firing up the old diesel, I consulted the GPS once more. It promised I would be at the park within two hours, well before sunset, leaving me more than enough time to set up camp. Satisfied, I headed along the now dirt road, eager to conquer the remaining miles.

The dirt road was good and smooth and I could feel the old Land Cruiser glide along contentedly. After ten miles, however, the road narrowed into a jeep track which was very uneven, with eroded gullies and tight turns. It led towards a jagged set of hills, rocky and dense with mopane forests, no settlements or villages in sight. Gradually the road wound its way deeper into the valley, eventually bringing me to an abrupt halt deep within the forest, a twenty-foot drop into a dry riverbed barring my way. The embankment was made up of steep, slick rock, with treacherous drop-offs on either side. Cutting the engine, I checked the GPS, zooming in as far as I could. I was, apparently, still on the right path. Clambering out of the vehicle for a closer inspection, I climbed down to the riverbed and was able to discern a manageable route. Back in the truck, a deep breath, tyres deflated and low range selected, I gingerly rolled over the edge.

The descent was little more than a controlled two-and-a-half-ton slide, but no damage was inflicted on the Cruiser... or, mostly no damage. The twin jeep tracks continued to cut through the rocky ravine and more descents into dry riverbeds followed. The going was slow, the rock-strewn path becoming narrower whilst the forest steadily grew denser. I still had 60 miles left to go and was now only averaging 12 miles per hour. There was no going back, however: the steep, slick riverbanks I had come down would be impossible to ascend and so, with the sun touching the crest of the iron hills to my right, I pushed on.

The track eventually spilt me out into a dried-up floodplain between the two ranges and led me through a village. It seemed as if the whole village came to a stop as I drove through, all eyes trained on this strange foreigner in his noisy truck. The road took me a little way out of the village and then stopped at a broad river. There I was met by four youths, varying in age from 12 to 16, all armed with AK-47s as they guarded their cattle. Immediately I could feel the anxiety building within me. I was alone in a well-stocked truck, unarmed and in the middle of the wilderness... and there were four of them armed to the teeth. Keeping calm, I gestured for them to approach, and, trying to hide my fear, asked for Luangwa. The eldest seemed to understand and gestured for me to go back to the village and turn right. Thanking him, I slowly reversed. Holding my breath all the while, I quickly headed back to the village.

At the village I found the turn-off he had referred to and headed back down the valley, but with the sunset quickly fading and the thought of encountering more youths with AK-47s, I was ill at ease. The road quickly deteriorated into a single track through tall fields of elephant grass which stretched skywards, almost three metres high. In disbelief I stopped to check the GPS again. Indifferent to my accusing glare, it insisted I was still on the right path. I turned my spotlights on only to be met by walls of thorn trees and elephant grass, which now surrounded me. The road, it seemed, had not been used in decades, and had become little more than a game trail. I had been driving for some 13 hours from Lusaka and as the darkness thickened around me I became very aware that I was truly alone and in all likelihood lost deep in the Zambian wilderness.

The thick grass tightened around the vehicle as I ploughed forward, scratching the paintwork like nails on a chalkboard, setting my nerves on edge. My sense of vulnerability deepened. So thick had the bush become that I could not open my door to get out. Opening my driver-side window to let in some fresh air saw leaves, branches, numerous insects, spiders and even a lizard emptied into my lap. Thorn trees pounded at the truck's bodywork, eventually tearing off both my windscreen wipers, but determinedly I pushed on. I looked at the GPS – still on the right path, it said, but the miles were now counting upwards... How was I moving further away from my goal? I cursed at it roundly, nerves taut, mind racing, dehydration starting to take its toll, but I didn't dare stop to take a drink. Five hours had passed since the Petauke turn-off and the road gave no respite. Then it suddenly disappeared altogether.

Before me lay another slow-moving river, stretching as far as my spotlights could shine. Memories of almost drowning my car in Botswana came flooding back. I would have to turn around after all, only I could not: the bush pushed up against the car so tightly I couldn't turn, I could only move forward. Panic began to set in. There was no one to reassure me, to ask advice of, no one to give a fresh perspective, just the darkness and a non-existent road. Forcing myself out of the car, I rolled up my trousers and waded in, not knowing if crocs or hippos might be lurking there in the dark. The river was only thigh deep, thankfully, and about 60 metres wide, and so, back in the vehicle, squinting and gnashing my teeth, I managed to get across it. I stopped for a minute on the other side and stared at the GPS... It was nine o'clock in the evening and I still had 50 miles to go.

After fighting my way through a particularly dense section of grass, I caught a glimpse of some movement to my right. Unsure if I had really seen something, I turned to look back through my rear-view mirror and struck something unseen. The Cruiser crashed to a halt while I was launched forward and hit the windscreen. I had hit a hidden tree stump! Dazed, I looked up and in the spotlights I saw two men approaching the car, with what looked like tall spears in their hands. My imagination primed after encountering the youths with AK-47s, and suspecting an ambush, I tried frantically to restart the truck. It spluttered back to life. Gunning the motor, I quickly reversed. Turning from the path, I plunged blindly into the sea of grass and raced around the men. Alone and surrounded by the dark and an unfamiliar landscape, my mind had became fertile ground for fear to take root, the sights and the sounds of the night feeding it all the while. I raced on, keen to escape my would-be attackers, my nerves shot as I bungled my way on through the night.

An hour later, the grassland gave way to a small open patch of woodland, a crescent moon visible through the thorn trees. Stopping the car, I grabbed my torch and got out to try to calm down and inspect the underside of the truck. I had hit the stump with my front right wheel, damaging the tie rod end. The steering was out but there were no leaks and nothing else looked broken – the old Cruiser could continue even if I could not. My nerves were raw, and even though logic dictated that no one would set an ambush on a road that had not been used in decades, using a tree stump no less, it still felt as if I was being pursued and so, getting back into the truck, I decided to push on.

Exhausted, I glanced at the small clock in the dashboard. It read eleven o'clock. Again I thought my mind was playing tricks on me when the bush around me began to move and sway. Turning off the engine, I stopped to listen. I could hear branches breaking and grass being crushed underfoot. Climbing out of my driver-side window, I clambered up on to the roof to look out over the walls of grass. Grey shapes slowly moved past me in the moonlight, dozens of them. I had driven into the midst of a herd of elephants. The sight of them milling about me was both exhilarating and terrifying. Quietly I watched, turning off all lights as the guardians of the forest moved past me, and for a moment I had a sense of how the world must have felt before the footprint of man arrived on the landscape. A sense of grace and equanimity scented the moonlit night as they passed by, completely at ease with the world. Half an hour later, the herd had moved on far enough for me to slowly creep forward once more. Thankfully the miles according to the GPS had begun to decrease once again; my destination, should I survive the night, was still thirty-odd miles away, my average speed eight miles per hour.

Midnight, and some new devilry to plague my progress. The road had become a very faint, but still very overgrown, jeep track once more. Across my path, plain to see in the spotlights, was a thick wire strung across the road between two tall fence posts. Exiting the car, I untied it and drove through, reconnecting the wire again before moving on. I encountered several more such wires across the path, each slowing me down horribly and adding to my ever-increasing sense of dread, but as long as I could move forward I was determined to do so. Then, in the faint moonlight, I began to see the silhouettes of huts in the distance and as I approached yet another wire barrier it dawned on me then that they were there to keep the elephants out of the villages. As I tried to untie the next wire across the path an electric shock jolted me backwards. To an observer it was comical, me landing squarely on my posterior like a cartoon character. However, fatigue, the intense concentration and the unknown which surrounded me had worn me down. The night threatened to nudge open the doors of delirium and delusion. I fetched two pairs of pliers from my truck and managed to undo the wire and drive through before reconnecting it without any further jolts to my system.

At the next wire I encountered, two youngsters were standing beside it: a toddler of about four years old and a boy of about fourteen. As I stopped, the eldest kindly undid the wire for me and approached my window before I drove through.

'Good evening, sir.' He smiled.

'You speak English?' I asked, my mouth agape, not trusting my mind.

'Yes, sir,' he replied. 'I teach English here in my village. My name is Stephen Perry.'

'It is good to meet you, Stephen,' I laughed with relief. 'I am Rudi. I am trying to get to South Luangwa, but the road is very bad.'

'Yes, sir, it was a road once, before I was born, but not now. It is very dangerous – there is too much elephants.'

'Yes,' I replied, 'I found a lot of them about ten miles back.'

'Very dangerous, sir, and it is very late. Please, why don't you rest here in my village? You can continue in the morning.'

It was almost midnight, I hadn't eaten since breakfast, my mind resembled a tangled-up fishing line, I was exhausted and was still seeing nothing but grass flickering in the spotlights even as I gazed into the friendly face of Stephen Perry, and so I accepted his gracious invitation.

Stephen led me into a clearing surrounded by mud huts, an old mopane tree in the middle of it, and in torchlight I quickly set up my tent beneath the old tree. Soon all the village kids and a good deal of the adults had come to see the *mzungu* who had got himself lost in the night. Intrigued, the children climbed in and out of the truck, fascinated by the various paraphernalia I was lugging around with me as I headed up the continent on my way to England. An immense sense of relief filled me then, seeing all those friendly faces lit up by the fire which had been made, and as we sat about it and talked, all my fear and doubt quickly fell away. Stephen dutifully translated for me as the elders asked about my trip and the children ran around playing, even though it was very late and a school night! Despite the hour and the fact these villagers were very poor, food was prepared for me and I was made to feel like one of the family.

At home we live behind walls and hide behind our mobile phones and move past each other like ghosts. But in the village everyone laughed and talked together, there was an acceptance, an honesty, a real sense of humanity, and of being present, which caught me completely off guard. Stephen had already adopted me as a long-lost brother and showed me around the village, his pleasant demeanour and infectious enthusiasm never fading. Eventually the excitement died down and parents ushered children back into their huts. Less than an hour before, my nerves had been frayed, my mind in a panic, but as I crawled into my tent and fell asleep, I felt happy and truly content.

I was awoken the next morning by the sound of chickens, one of whose relatives I had dined on the previous night. Stephen Perry was already up and about and greeted me with that same big smile. He helped me pack up my tent, brought me some water to wash with and asked if I would give him and some of the other children a lift to the school. Soon the inside of the truck, the bonnet and the roof were packed with some 20 children, all holding on for dear life, laughing and screaming as we bounced along the uneven dirt track at three miles per hour. I thanked Stephen for his generous hospitality, and gave him a handful of pens as a small gesture of my appreciation (you never give sweets to village children – dentists are few and far between in the bush so pens are much more valuable!). Then I took my leave and headed out on the path for Luangwa once more.

Another four hours of driving saw me reach South Luangwa National Park, and though the road remained horrendous, being able to negotiate it in daylight made it an adventure rather than a fight for survival. Some ten months later, after crossing Africa, the Middle East and Europe, I finally crossed the Channel and arrived in London. I had known from the start that I would face some of my greatest fears on the trip, but it hadn't been malaria, a rabid beast or some ruthless gang of bandits that had been the cause of my greatest fears. It had been a road – the road from Petauke – and what had saved me from the nightmare was the smiling face of a boy out there in the bush, named Stephen Perry. I think of him often, and hope that he is still happy and well, and that he knows that the evening I spent with him and his family beneath the African moon in their small village will remain with me always.

ABOUT RUDI

In the navy Rudi was fortunate enough to visit many memorable places, including Marion Island, St Helena, Turkey and Bangladesh. Sailing across the Indian and Atlantic Oceans instilled a burning desire to travel and see as much of this breathtaking planet as he possibly could. Fascinated by the natural world and the astonishing biodiversity with which we share this planet, Rudi is particularly drawn to the tranquillity of mountains and deserts, with the Namib and Wadi Rum being two of his favourite places in the world.

When he is not travelling, Rudi is also a keen photographer (inspired from a young age by the countless stacks of *National Geographic* in his parents' modest library), reader and writer. There is, after all, no greater thing than life, and we are fortunate enough to share it with a world teeming with so many miraculous forms of it!

Find out more about Rudi at:

W: africanclipper@tumblr.com

26

AT DAY'S END

We are a part of all
that we have met

Sarah Outen

Thunder rumbled across grey skies, air thickly humid and clouds ripe with rain. Dusk edged closer as I pushed to squeeze the last miles from a long day. I was mud-covered and sweaty.

Please let there be somewhere to buy food, I thought as I stood up on my pedals to push myself into the village, wheels sliding in the mud. Happily there was a small shop. I smiled as I walked in and the gathered group of noisy card players fell silent in surprise. I was not their regular customer, apparently. Eyes flitted between me and my bike outside as the previously unheard TV now held the airtime, before chatter raced back and forth again. I had hoped to nip in, buy something to eat and fill up my water and then get going as quickly as possible to find a place to pitch my tent before dark.

I answered the torrent of questions as best I could, while making a little pile of food on the counter. The young Chinese girl smiled at me as she totted up the bill. To my surprise she gave me the total in English, with a bashful smile and wide dark eyes.

Her father appeared at her shoulder and intercepted my hand as I passed a handful of paper bills over. My eyes met his and he beamed at me, saying something in Chinese which I didn't understand. The look and returned bills told me that he didn't want my money and I found myself swallowing back tears.

The questions and Chinese translation of what they thought my answers must mean flowed on. They roared with laughter when I gestured that I would be camping tonight, and then jaws dropped when they realised I was serious. After some persuasion, I accepted their insistent offer that I stay with them for the night. Before I knew it, I had been ushered through the courtyard, shown the long drop and the bathroom, and in spite of my assurance that I would have been happy pitching my tent in the yard, the young daughter had been moved out of her bedroom so that I could have her bed. I gave my English–Chinese dictionary to the daughter, an aspiring medical student, when I left the next morning, fuelled by a hearty breakfast and the warmth of being among a family.

Similar versions of this story were not uncommon on my journey to pedal, paddle and row around the northern hemisphere. People often seemed to be handing me on along the road – a journey to which they would probably never know the ending or the outcome but, for the moments or miles where our paths crossed, they were adding strength to my reserves, either practically or emotionally. They all became a part of the story, threading together the miles and memories, as in Tennyson's 'Ulysses', where he declares 'I am a part of all that I have met'.

The power of kindness is huge, infinite maybe. And, similarly for gratitude – the companion of kindness – remembering and cultivating both makes us more open, more able to give and receive. It feels like now, more than ever, we would all do well to be more open and kind, rather than building walls or creating policies to make it harder to welcome and share and connect.

ABOUT SARAH

Sarah Outen is an adventurer, author and speaker. In November 2015 she completed her London2London: Via the World challenge. The 4.5-year expedition saw her row, cycle and kayak over 20,000 miles, starting and finishing at Tower Bridge, albeit with a few diversions and changes to the original plan.

Sarah loves wild places and the transformative effect of time spent outside. She has written two books about her adventures: *A Dip in the Ocean* and *Dare to Do*.

Find out more about Sarah at:

W: www.sarahouten.com ◆ T: @SarahOuten

27

FOOTFALL

Wild camping alone in the
Andes, a cyclist can't hide

Stephen Fabes

F ootfall?

Muscles go taut. I'm swaddled in a sleeping bag, my body as tensioned and tremulous as a tightrope walker. It's a familiar paralysis. Roadside camping brings an anxiety that feels primal, that lives in my guts. This firing of synapses probably saved some distant ancestor, in a more dangerous epoch, when sabretooths roved the plains. Stray dogs and nosy kids are the rovers now. But my pulse still quickens. It can't be reasoned with; it won't be assuaged.

I lie still, barely breathing, letting the soundscape of the night run in. The wind tugs at my tent. I can't hear any footsteps now. *Perhaps I never did.* A dream maybe, or the fidgeting of trees: the innocent pretence of boughs knocking against one another in the night.

The blue glow of my watch says 3 a.m. Momentarily, I'm lost. My brain zooms in like I'm moving a cursor on Google Maps: South America, Peru, somewhere in La Sierra. I've been cycling around the world for three years now, and nights can blend together. Disorientation is as sure as sunrise.

The previous evening comes back to me now in a hail of fragments. Backcountry. The clustered lights of a small town on the far side of the valley, ages away by bicycle. I remember coming to a house. It stood aloof and derelict; a concrete place, long-shadowed and as empty as I'd hoped when I peered in through the hole in the wall where a window should have been. The tin roof jutted out beyond the outside walls, providing three feet of shelter. A choice spot for a tent as ratty and punched by holes as mine; a chance to escape the worst of the rain.

Rough camping is often haunted by stray sounds and grumbling portents. Camping between towns, in the edgeland, can feel as heady as camping in wild and unpeopled places. I've left a long trail of nights behind me, hidden myself in half-light and jumbled shrubs, aside droning roadsides where car headlights tear strips into the night and street lights wink with the witchery of stars.

There's a feeling – during these nightly detours – of stalking society. It's thrillingly outsiderish: I'm the thief at the window. Childishly fun, like a game of hide-and-seek. The world threatens to out me, and beyond my tent it's a presence, with intent; pestering, making a fuss. The clanks of industry are chattering teeth. The pylons hiss like vipers. The farm dogs harangue: have they found my scent?

It's easy enough to find a patch of earth to make my own campsite, but I fancy myself an expert now. Most nights have melted from memory, though a few I recall as glorious victories: the Jordanian clifftop, the Californian sea cave, the middle of a French roundabout, the ramparts of a ruined Ottoman castle. Others I remember as stonking defeats, and these I've catalogued under labels which invoke time-worn horror movies – *The Night of the Fire Ants*, *The Dawn of the Scorpion under my Therm-a-Rest* and *The Midnight of the Flood*. When the footfall is not the axe-murdering sociopath you know it must be, you experience a sense of escape that washes away all of that gut-sunken fear and seems to make the whole process ecstatically worth it.

Crunch crunch.

Shit.

Crunch.

I've been here before too, the moment that doubt dissolves. The feet – I'm sure now – are pacing out a careful circle. I'm being considered. I'm being surveyed. My visitor turns back and crunches to the other side of my tent. Nothing for it now – I'm busted. The footsteps are too close, too precise.

I revive myself in a jolt, unzip my tent and peer out. Blackness. And then the intimation of someone, a dim silhouette. The figure moves, faster, faster, long strides, and I'm staring at knees and he bends down and then: eyes, and something in his right hand, and shit shit shit it looks like a gun. He levels it. It's aimed at my head.

It's a black pistol. It gleams metallically. It looks illusory and weird. Something inside me falls and stays falling. I'm not breathing.

Talk.

I'm babbling. Spanish comes in a messy flood, words clambering over themselves, pronunciation gone to shit.

'I'm a traveller, it was raining, I needed somewhere out of the rain. What's your name? I'm Stephen. You don't need the gun.'

'*Fuera*' – Get out. Not angry, not calm. Just instructive. I move. It happens in a flurry; I've twisted out of my sleeping bag, my shorts are on, I'm scrabbling to leave my tent. I'm saying 'crap' a lot. And now I'm standing in front of a man with a revolver pointed at my guts. I can see the terrain of his face now; he's wet with rain. His eyes punch into me; they're wide and alert. His cheeks are streaked with mud. I'm shaking. He's shaking too. His gun hand wavers.

I'm consoled a little: he's scared. I hope that it matters. But scared enough to do something rash? I feel myself spiralling again. He angles the gun up a little; a bullet would punch through my chest. My lungs, my heart, my aorta, my spinal cord.

'You get in. Get into my house!' There's a tremble in that voice too.

OK, it's *his* house. *Think, think.* But I'm numb. My mind's snagged.

Who is he? One of the infamous *ladrones* perhaps, the bandits of village lore. There's a flash of a conversation I had three weeks ago with another cyclist who'd been shot at; he'd shown me where a bullet had grazed his bicycle frame. It had sounded so fantastical I'd chosen not to believe him. Or maybe he's one of the *rondas campesinas*, the local vigilantes who patrol rural Peru and fill in for the police – that would be better.

I walk towards the front door of the house, too fast. He follows shortly behind me, the footfall worse than before. I feel the tendons in my neck, I listen for a shot and wait for my back to explode, for blood to soak the front of my chest, movie-style. I reach the wooden door and it creaks open under my shove.

He follows me in and lights a gas lamp. A room speeds into view. A sparse place. There's a table, two stools and a stove in the corner that I must have missed when I'd peered in last night, but there's little else to suggest this is anyone's home. He motions for me to sit.

'What do you want?' he says.

That flustered zip of his eyes, that catch in his voice.

'I'm just a tourist, from England. I'm travelling by bicycle. I needed somewhere to camp. The rain...'

His eyes fall away from me and make circles on the floor. He scrunches up his face; he seems to be thinking.

'It's cold tonight,' he says at last.

'*Si, señor.*'

'*¿Quieres sopa?*'

Would I like some soup?

I think so.

'*¿Pollo o tomate?*'

'*Qué?*'

'*Tengo pollo o tomate.*'

I like chicken, and I like tomato. But I go off-menu.

'Can you put the gun down?'

He does so, with a dawning smile. With the gun on the sill, he moves over to the stove and fiddles, his back to me. The gun is beyond an intrepid lunge away, I notice.

He returns with two bowls of tomato soup and places one in front of me. It steams gently. He takes a seat too, and we begin to eat.

'Men came to my home last month. They had guns. They took everything,' he says, flapping a hand at his spartan home. 'I bought this for protection. I didn't know who you were. I thought you might be one of them.'

He smiles and I realise I'm doing the same, but in a wildly exaggerated way.

'I knocked,' I mumble. 'There was nobody in. Why are you back so late?'

'*Oro,*' he says. *Gold.*

Everything slots into place. The hour, the muddy face, all those holes I'd noted cut deep into the hillsides. He's been mining. It's illegal, save for the multinationals, but local men ignore the rules and make nocturnal forays.

'Look what I found.' He digs into his pocket and brings out a wad of tissue paper. Opening it up, two nuggets glint in the wander of the gaslight.

We talk, Asto and I. He tells me about his family – a wife and three young children who live in a poor industrial town on the coast. The money from the gold will look after them. He describes the makeshift mines, his best finds, the occasional cave-ins.

Finally, he takes my bowl. 'If you need anything, you can knock. *Buenas noches, señor.*'

'*Muchas gracias,*' I say, with as much feeling as I can muster.

I walk back to my tent. The rain has stopped and a few stars are out. I wrap myself in my sleeping bag, and fall asleep slowly next to Asto's home, sensitive again to the murmurings of the night. There's a lulling whisper to the wind, and in a few hours the sun will rise.

Footsteps again, as the sun fires up my tent. And a voice: '*¡Esteban! ¡Esteban!*'

I peer out and see Asto: he's grinning. And he's holding a steaming bowl of tomato soup: I'm getting breakfast in bed.

'To give you strength for your journey, *señor*. I wish you luck in my country. Please, be safe.'

ABOUT
STEPHEN

Stephen Fabes is a medical doctor, writer, storyteller and adventure cyclist. Like most decisions of great consequence, his plan to cycle around the world was made in a pub, beer in one hand, mini atlas in the other. He spent more than six years spanning 75 countries on six continents, crossing remote cloud forests in Myanmar and frozen lakes in Mongolia, the mountains of the Caucasus and the deserts of Syria and Afghanistan. He cycled 86,209 kilometres – a distance equivalent to more than twice around the world.

En route Stephen visited remote medical projects serving those on the margins of society. His writing has appeared in *The Guardian*, *The Telegraph*, the BBC, CNN, *Geographical*, *Adventure Travel*, *Backpacker* and *Wild* among others. His first book is forthcoming.

———

Find out more about Stephen at:
W: www.cyclingthe6.com
T: @cyclingthe6 ✦ F: @Cyclingthe6

28
KINDNESS AS REBELLION

In a world where headlines encourage us to fear anyone different, one woman discovered, by chance, a universal language of kindness

Tina Brocklebank

In October 2015 I went to volunteer in Calais for a week. Sixteen months later I finally left. People ask me why I went in the first place and my answer is always the same. Up until that point crises like this happened somewhere else, half a world away, to people I didn't know or didn't think I could connect with. But the geography of global crises is changing and I found it impossible to know that this was right on our doorstep and do nothing. People then ask why I stayed so long, but that question has many more answers. The crux of it was similar, I guess, in that I couldn't see what I had seen in that first week, meet the people I had met, and then just return to my cosy life as if that week had never happened. I remember being struck by such an overwhelming feeling of solidarity among all the volunteers, an astonishing energy that coalesced from people being drawn together to be a collective 'No' to the injustice that was unfolding in front of our eyes and in our backyard. Volunteers had left their lives and jobs in the UK and were working so damn hard, not for any monetary recompense but because, very simply, they wanted to *be* a difference. History was being written right there in Calais; in the smuggler-run lorry parks where men, women and children tried night after night to hide in the lorries and on the disused landfill site that became home to thousands of people the world didn't want to see. I remember thinking that the history books would judge us on this place and what happened there. With all this in mind, staying for 16 months made complete sense. I have rarely felt more sure about anything in my life. It was compelling for all the right reasons.

A friend once suggested the idea of 'kindness as a rebellion' to me; an insurgent mutiny of compassion battling against the dominant narrative of fear-mongering and prejudice-fuelled hate. It seems astonishing that kindness could be seen as a revolutionary rebellious act. Yet, as a volunteer working with hundreds of other volunteers in a space where organisations were wholly absent, where states could think only of fences, miles of barbed wire and walls, kindness in Calais was a currency prized above almost everything else. There were a million acts of kindness in Calais every day; acts that demonstrated solidarity and compassion. Acts that said, 'I see you as more than the anonymous label of "refugee"; I see you.' Acts that communicated breathtaking love and humble generosity. There was no place for sedated denial in Calais; demonstrating kindness to a stranger required us to recognise another's suffering and need and respond. It obliged us to acknowledge a shared humanity, a togetherness of humankind. It's no coincidence that kindness starts with 'kin'. The tragedy and desperation that continues to unfold in Calais every day is so challenging; it's incredibly uncomfortable and it hurts so much to see it. Yet if we look away from the hard bits we become blind to the reality for another one of us. If all this meant we were renegades waging war on indifference and prejudice with tools of smiles, compassion and kindness then so be it. I was more than happy to be part of that uprising.

The moment I decided that I had to give up my UK life and return to Calais long term came when I drove into the camp with fellow volunteers for the first time. At this point refugees were arriving 24 hours a day; shaping and filling a space that would become known as the Jungle. The disused landfill site and nearby sand dunes were slowly being covered in a multicoloured patchwork of nylon and tarpaulin as people claimed and cleared a space for tents. As we drove along pitted, puddle-filled tracks, tired figures carried children and tattered bags of possessions, having just arrived; others picked their way in flip-flops through mud and rubbish to queue at insufficient, uncovered water points, their weary bodies expressing a desperate physical and emotional exhaustion that words could never articulate. 'The most important thing you can give here is your smile,' said a fellow volunteer sitting next to me. I have never forgotten that moment. *That* simple comment is why I stayed 16 months.

If you had told me a year, a month or even a week before October 2015 that I would spend almost a year and a half developing and coordinating food distribution systems in a refugee camp in northern France, I would have laughed in your face. I didn't know anything about food distribution or refugees in or out of camps. I had never met people from Afghanistan, Syria, Iran, Sudan, Iraq, Eritrea, Ethiopia or Kuwait before. I couldn't speak Arabic, Pashto, Farsi or Tigrinya. I knew nothing of coordinating humanitarian aid or appealing for donations or responding to such urgent need. It came as an enormous surprise to me that when it came down to it, none of that actually mattered. The one and only thing that did matter, however, was that these extraordinarily brave, resilient, gracious people deserved dignity and respect. They deserved compassion and humanity. They deserved kindness, for no other reason than that we all deserve kindness. But the world these people were fleeing was one of war and persecution and the world they had journeyed to was one of border fences and exclusion. Their journeys were punctuated by exploitative people smugglers, Libyan prisons, unsafe boats, violent border-security guards, barbed wire, rubber bullets and tear gas. Their appearance and demeanour in the Calais Jungle conveyed their desperate disillusionment at the unfriendly Europe they had travelled so far to find safety and refuge in. But the effect of simply making eye contact and smiling was astonishing. It was possible to visibly see people stand taller, a previously defeated face brighten as if suddenly injected with the possibility of hope – all from a smile given by a stranger. Because once you have exchanged a smile you aren't strangers any more.

This simple human interaction never stopped being so powerful and I never stopped being amazed at how much was communicated through such a small gesture. We were all strangers in the Jungle in the beginning, volunteers and refugees alike, joined together in this extraordinary place. Volunteers came from far and wide, for a single afternoon, a week or for months at a time. Our 'Jungle family' was an all-inclusive community, where volunteers arrived, found a job that needed doing and just got on with it. There was no recruitment, no interviews, no person specification or skill criteria for specific tasks, though maybe in hindsight some of this would have been helpful! Instead people just turned up, were welcomed and allocated a job. No one stayed a stranger for long. The longer you stayed the more responsibility you got and we learned by trial and error how best to organise donations and distributions. Days in camp were full of a million human exchanges, hundreds of greetings in Arabic and Pashto, obligatory handshakes with everyone, hugs with many, countless smiles and so much said through eye contact. Where language can be a barrier, these physical connections and this wordless communication were so powerful. People called out 'Jungle Mama!' – a mark of respect (I think!) for having been there so long distributing food, or '*Makina!*' – an Arabic word meaning 'machine' or 'one who works without stopping'. Affectionate shouts of 'Hey, *lemonay!*' – Pashto for 'crazy'. There was so much banter, so much playfulness, so much warmth. We received endless invites into cramped tents or small shelters with dirt floors to share tea with people that had so little and yet were so rich in grace and generosity. People would collect their food parcels and then instantly open their one packet of biscuits to share. There was an enormous shared sense of belonging and of shared experience. I have spoken to many refugees and volunteers since the camp was evicted and cleared and this bond is even stronger than before. Our experience was a shared moment in both history and geography, and it had a culture, community and language all of its own.

The big difference was that the rest of the world seemed to be speaking a completely different language. An ugly narrative dominated; one that cast refugees as 'other', as a threat to national values and identity and, even worse, as terrorists. People as brothers, mothers, fathers, sons, grandfathers and grandmothers alike were lost in the dehumanising semantics of determining people in need as 'economic migrant' or 'refugee', at the same time as lives were being lost in the Mediterranean and being held in a barbed-wire-enclosed limbo at closed borders. A contemporary moral panic is currently nurtured by politicians and the media alike; the refugee epitomises everything we are encouraged to fear and vilify, someone that looks different, dresses differently and speaks differently. If this difference is accompanied by a burkha or a headscarf then they are certainly seen as someone to be feared and excluded. But this fear is rarely if ever generated by direct personal experience; it is fostered by those who have something to gain from our mistrust and anxiety. Look beyond the xenophobic narrative of the 'swarms, floods and marauders' that apparently threaten to draw our national moral compass off course and you find... people. That's it. People, just like us. Only, not quite like us, because we have the golden ticket of a European passport which means if we go to live abroad we are labelled an expat, not a migrant. The geographical lottery of birth determines the world we are born into and this in turn determines the language that articulates our personal story. A tale told in words of inclusion or exclusion; kindness or cruelty; friends or strangers.

My experiences in Calais brought me face-to-face, hand-to-hand with thousands of strangers. While so much of the world classifies these as the 'other' I am meant to fear, I have encountered 'other' as only like myself. Because whether I am a 45-year-old white, Western, divorced woman from Yorkshire or a 26-year-old single man from Afghanistan my experience taught me that we have far more in common than whatever divides us. Overwhelmingly I met people with the same values, the same hopes, the same dreams as myself. I learned that we respond in the same way to the same stimuli, whether that stimulus is a smile or a scream, an act of kindness or of conflict.

The sociologist Frank Furedi writes of a 'culture of fear' that is fostered by headlines and policy agenda – in other words, a fear that is socially constructed. So, if this fear is created and manufactured, surely the possibility exists for us to redraft the dominant narrative and construct an alternative? As did hundreds of others, I poured my heart and soul into Calais and into rewriting the ugly script that overshadows the truth and reality of people's stories. It was impossible for me to see, hear and feel people's experiences and not do that. These people are like you and me. Only, they are not. Generally they are ignored and judged and despised by much of the world. They are treated as inconvenient by our government and assumed to be terrorists when in reality they are themselves fleeing terrorism and violence. They want what you and I have – peace, safety and opportunity. They want Kindness. And to not be seen as a Stranger.

ABOUT TINA

Tina currently works for a small but beautifully formed charity supporting refugees and asylum seekers in Leeds (www.lassn.org. uk). She is also studying for an MA in Refugee Protection and Forced Migration Studies. Before going to Calais, she spent 24 years working with children, young people and families in a wide variety of roles both nationally and internationally. Tina is an avid cycle-tourist and has cycled from the top to the bottom of New Zealand and completed solo trips across Europe and in the UK. At age 47, she recently took up running and is about to complete her second half-marathon.

ABOUT OXFAM'S WORK WITH REFUGEES

By buying this book, you're doing something life-saving. You're supporting refugees around the world.

———

Imagine if your life – your home, your livelihood, your community – was destroyed in the chaos of conflict or disaster. Imagine if you and your family had to run for your lives with just the clothes you were wearing, at the terrifying moment your world fell apart. For more than 65 million people worldwide, these unimaginable situations have become a daily reality.

But the kindness of people like you is bringing hope. By buying this book, you're helping to get safe water to women, men and children in Syria and the thousands sheltering in the world's largest refugee camp in Uganda. You're making it possible to build sanitation systems to keep people healthy in camps in Lebanon, Jordan and Tanzania. You're providing food for the people who would otherwise go hungry in South Sudan. You're helping refugees the world over to know and understand their rights.

It's a worldwide crisis. Closer to home, Oxfam supporters have helped provide warm clothes, food and toiletries – as well as legal aid and advice – for people arriving in Greece, Italy, Macedonia and Serbia. The vast number of people who are now displaced, having been forced to flee terrifying conflict, poverty or disaster, is one of the defining challenges of our time. Thank you so much for being there and standing as one with refugees.

To find out about other ways you can help, and learn about Oxfam's work beating poverty around the world, visit **www.oxfam.org.uk**

HOW YOU CAN HELP

All of the royalties from the sales of this book are going directly to Oxfam's work with refugees, but there are many other great charities doing important work with refugees around the world that also need our help. If you would like to help, either by volunteering your time, fundraising, sending money or collecting clothes then please get in touch with one of the following charities, or search online – there are lots of brilliant projects raising money for specific crises and all need support:

CalAid
www.calaid.co.uk
CalAid is a grassroots charity who were the largest provider of non-food items in the Epirus region but who now focus on providing free eye tests and glasses to refugees and displaced people in Greece. They also provide baby kits to expectant mums with all the essentials they'll need to care for their child.

Help Refugees
www.helprefugees.org
Help Refugees is the biggest facilitator of grassroots humanitarian aid in Europe, funding more than 80 projects across Europe and the Middle East. With no highly paid executives, the money goes directly where it's needed, with small but effective groups and organisations responding where the need is greatest to provide food, clothing, shelter and funding quickly and effectively.

Utopia 56
www.utopia56.com/en
Utopia 56 was created in early 2016 to gather and coordinate volunteers to help refugees in northern France, both in Paris and Calais. They collaborate with other existing organisations to organise 2,700 volunteering days a month, distributing clothing, meals, blankets and medical care and organising activities for refugees.

Leeds Asylum Seekers' Support Network
www.lassn.org.uk/
Leeds Asylum Seekers' Support Network was set up in 1999 to offer friendship and practical help including counselling and psychotherapy to refugees and asylum seekers in the area.

Go to **bit.ly/AidResourceMap** to find your closest drop-off point for clothes and shoes to be donated to refugees. Some charities will also take donations of dictionaries, musical instruments, books, camping equipment, sanitary items, mobile phones and food.

You can find more information at
www.storiesthatmakeyourheartgrow.com.

ACKNOWLEDGEMENTS

The team at Kindness of Strangers would like to thank and acknowledge the contributions of the following people, all of whom have helped with the Kindness of Strangers project. Without you, this book wouldn't have been possible.

Sheonah Howlett ✦ Monica Bidoli ✦ Natasha Khan
Gergana Adams ✦ The team at Sliced Events
Caroline Georges ✦ Emma Crossley ✦ The team at Oxfam
Faye Singer-Clark ✦ Barry Causton and the team at Oxjam
Islington ✦ Nish Saccaran ✦ Paul Glynn ✦ Caitriona O'Connor
Mark Bennet ✦ Josh Tinsely ✦ Angelica Yiacoupis
Alastair Humpreys ✦ Julian Sayarer ✦ Mark Kalch
Leon McCarron ✦ Ed Stafford ✦ Anna McNuff ✦ Levison Wood
Pip Stewart ✦ Jamie McDonald ✦ Debbie Chapman
Emily Chappell ✦ Angela Wilson ✦ Katie Arnold
Easkey Britton ✦ Tom Lowe and the team at FourPure
Toby Sims ✦ Breifne Earley ✦ Becky Lamb ✦ Joby Lubman
Lucy Haken ✦ Sarah Outen ✦ Jo Cantello ✦ Elise Downing
Amelia Burr ✦ Lindsey Cole ✦ Faraz Shibli ✦ Dr Stephen Fabes
Lois Pryce ✦ Benedict Allen ✦ Laura & Tim Moss ✦ Sarah Little
Hannah Engelkamp ✦ Tina Brockleback ✦ Rebecca Lowe
George Martin ✦ Sue Martin ✦ Thomas Martin
Aine O'Nuallain ✦ Maura Clesham ✦ Niall O'Nuallain
Finn O'Nuallain ✦ Rudi Stark ✦ James Borrell
George Mahood ✦ Lilly Quinn ✦ Charlie Carroll
Simon Evans ✦ Hannah Silvester

COPYRIGHT ACKNOWLEDGEMENTS

Have you enjoyed this book?
If so, why not write a review on your
favourite website?

If you're interested in finding out more
about our books, find us on Facebook at
Summersdale Publishers and follow us
on Twitter at **@Summersdale**.

Thanks very much for buying this
Summersdale book.

www.summersdale.com